Classical Ornament

C. THIERRY

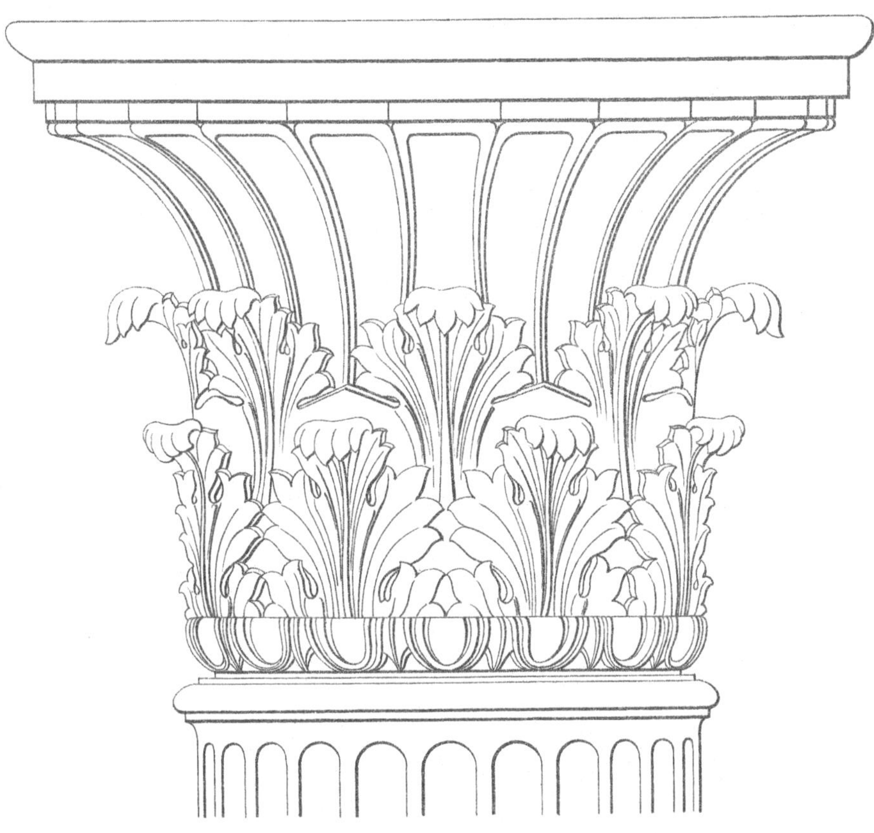

Dover Publications, Inc.
Mineola, New York

The decorative arts of Ancient Greece and Rome—richly ornate and characterized by mythological creatures, floral borders, and graceful engravings—were especially remarkable for the complex yet fluid nature of their design and their inspired craftsmanship. This fascinating volume presents more than 70 illustrations of classical ornament, consisting of architectural elements from structures such as the Parthenon, the Acropolis, the Vatican Museum, and other buildings.

Originally compiled in the 1860s, the book is filled with precisely detailed renderings of doors, windows, decorative stonework, columns, pedestals, headstones, and more. It remains a richly varied resource of authentic images of classical ornament, ideal for students of architecture and the decorative arts and essential for graphic artists and designers in search of royalty-free illustrations.

Bibliographical Note

Classical Ornament, first published by Dover Publications, Inc., in 2016, contains all the plates from *Classiche Ornamente,* originally published by J. Veith, Carlsruhe, Germany, ca. 186–.

DOVER *Pictorial Archive* SERIES

International Standard Book Number

ISBN-13: 978-0-486-79965-0
ISBN-10: 0-486-79965-4

Manufactured in the United States by RR Donnelley
79965401 2016
www.doverpublications.com

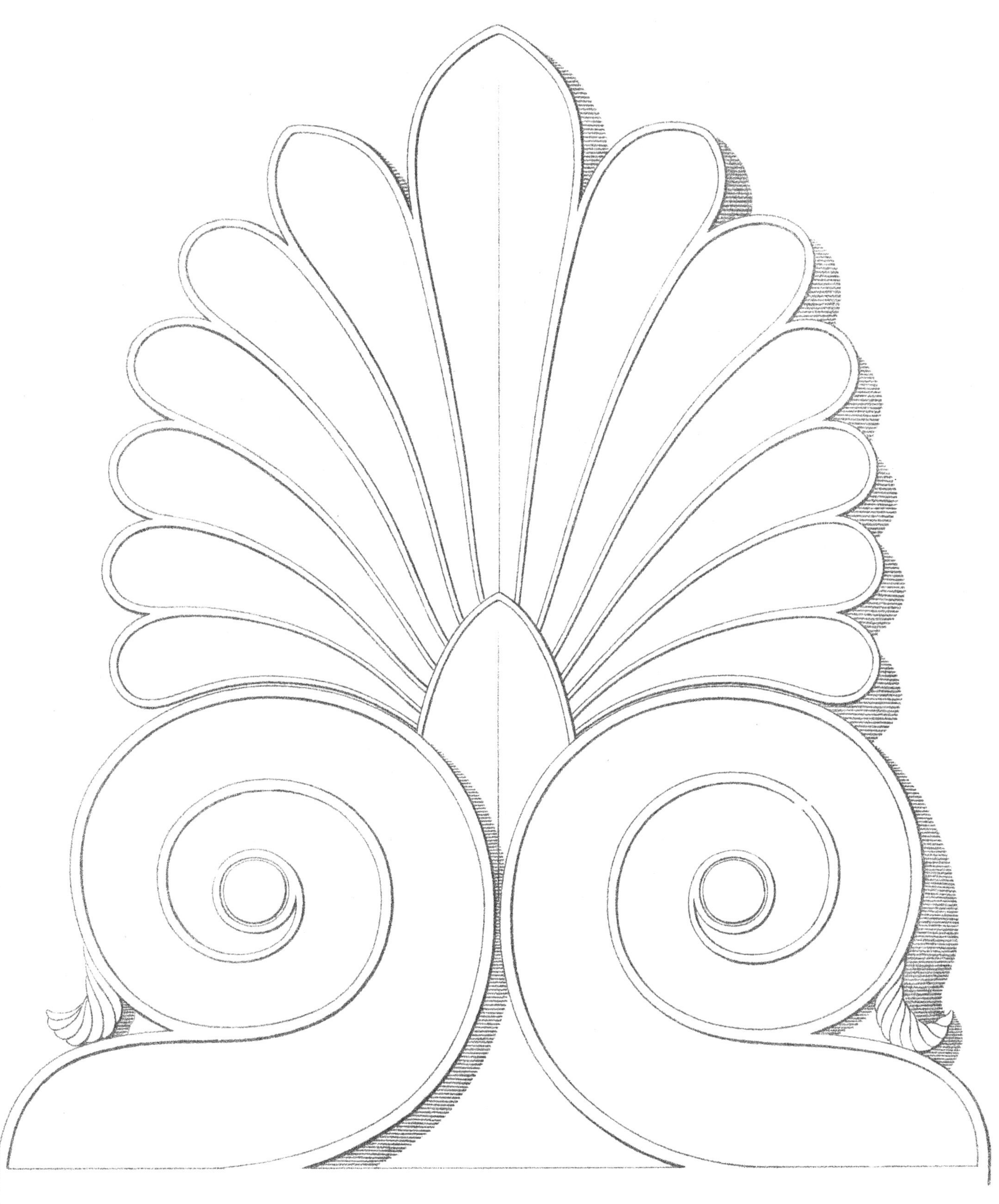

Marble ornament on the Parthenon

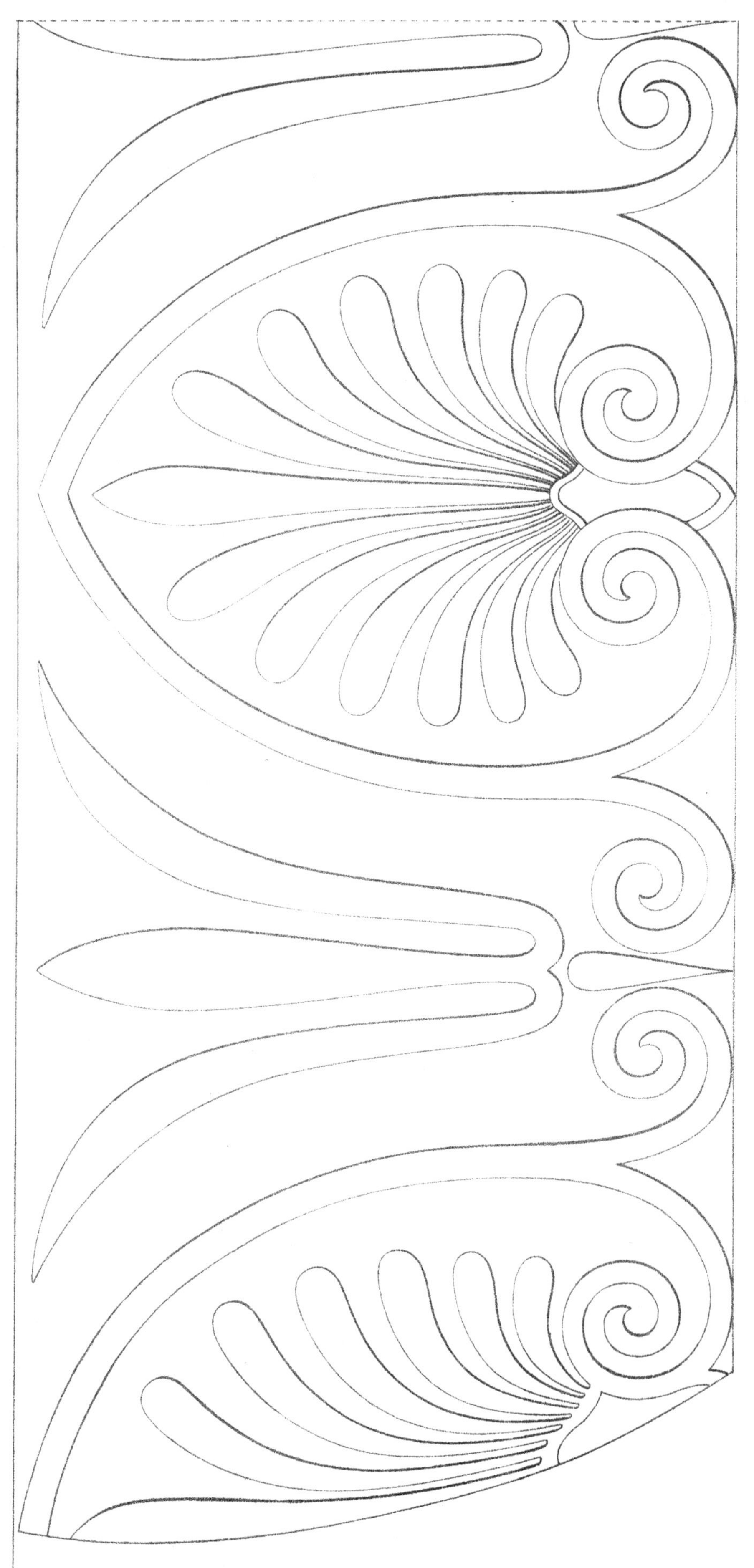

Plate 2

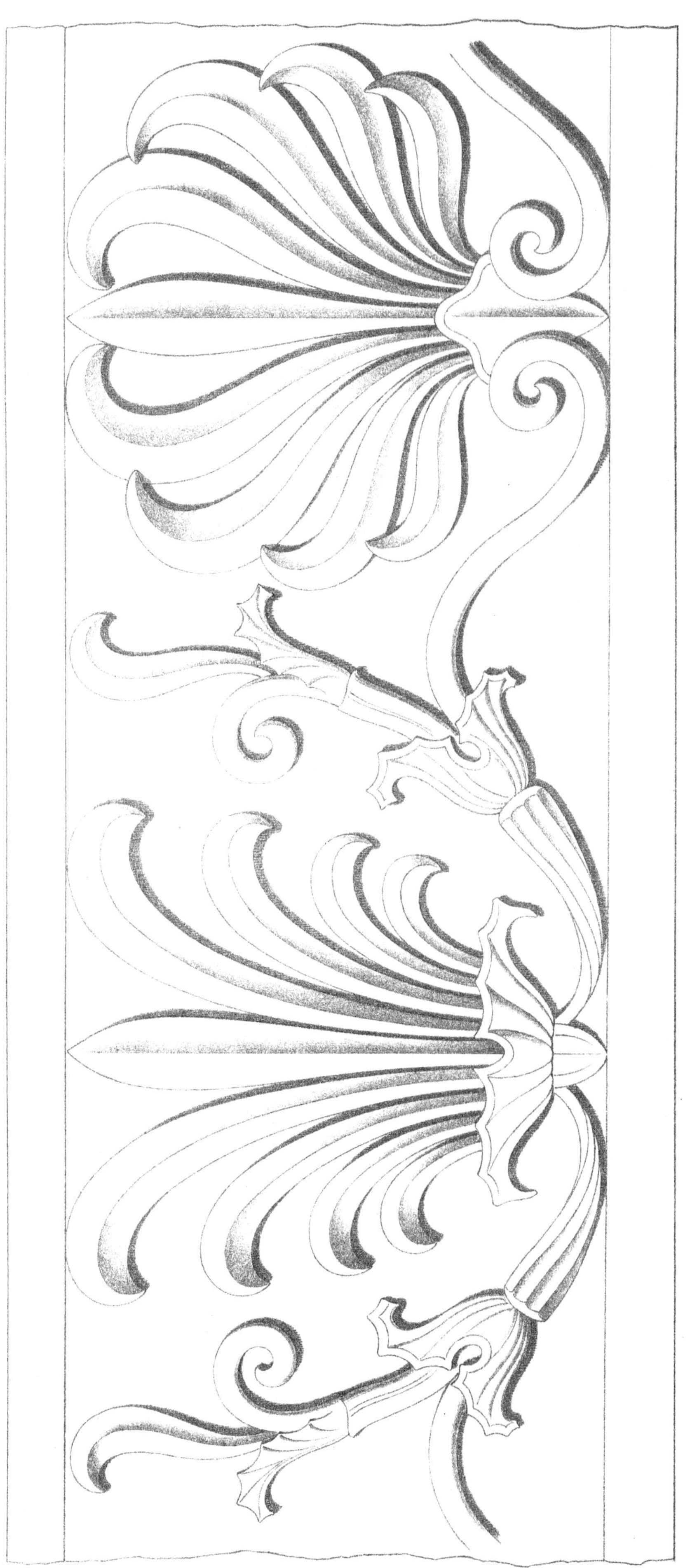

Plate 3

PLATE 4

Decoration on the Temple of Erechtheus in Athens

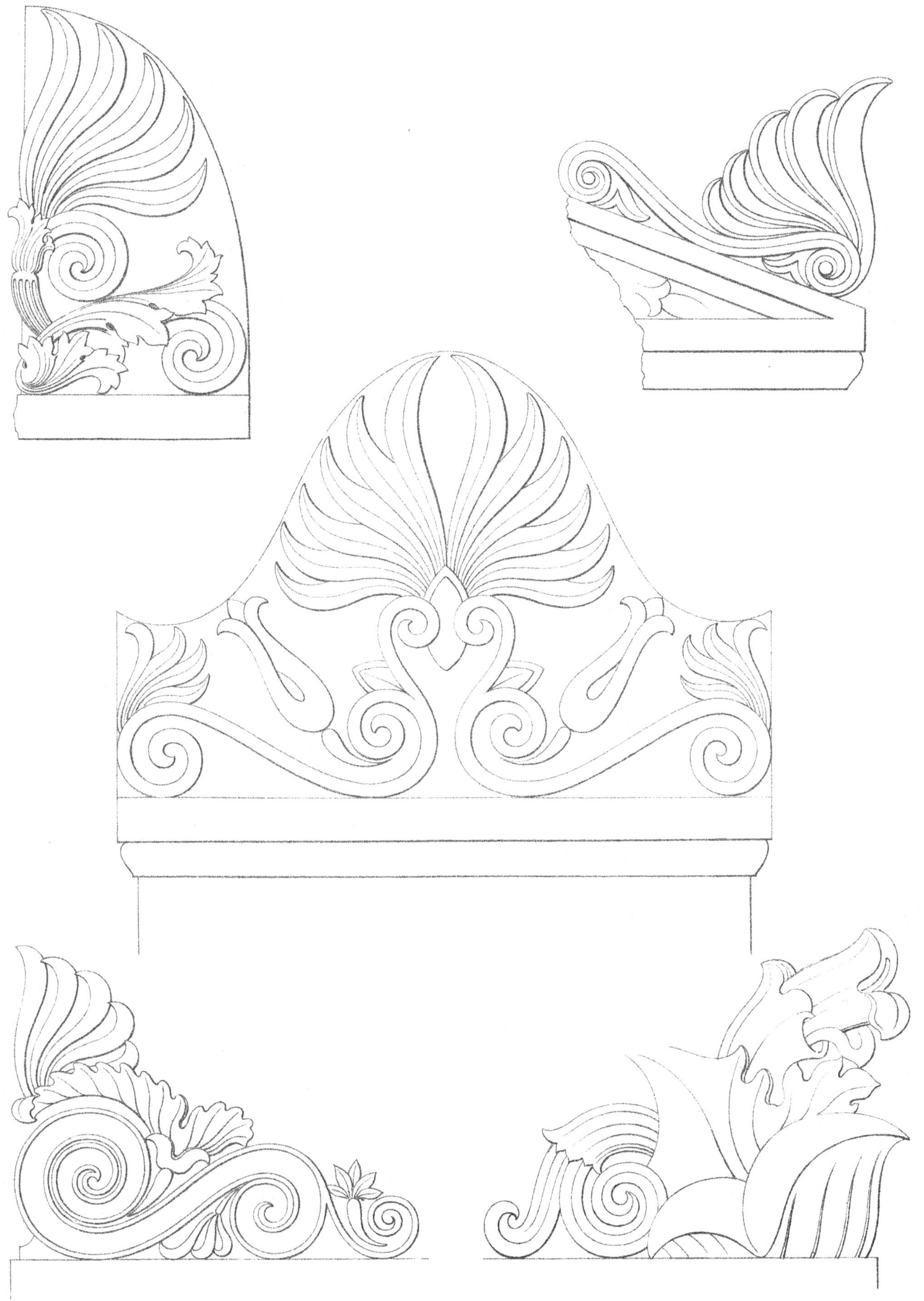

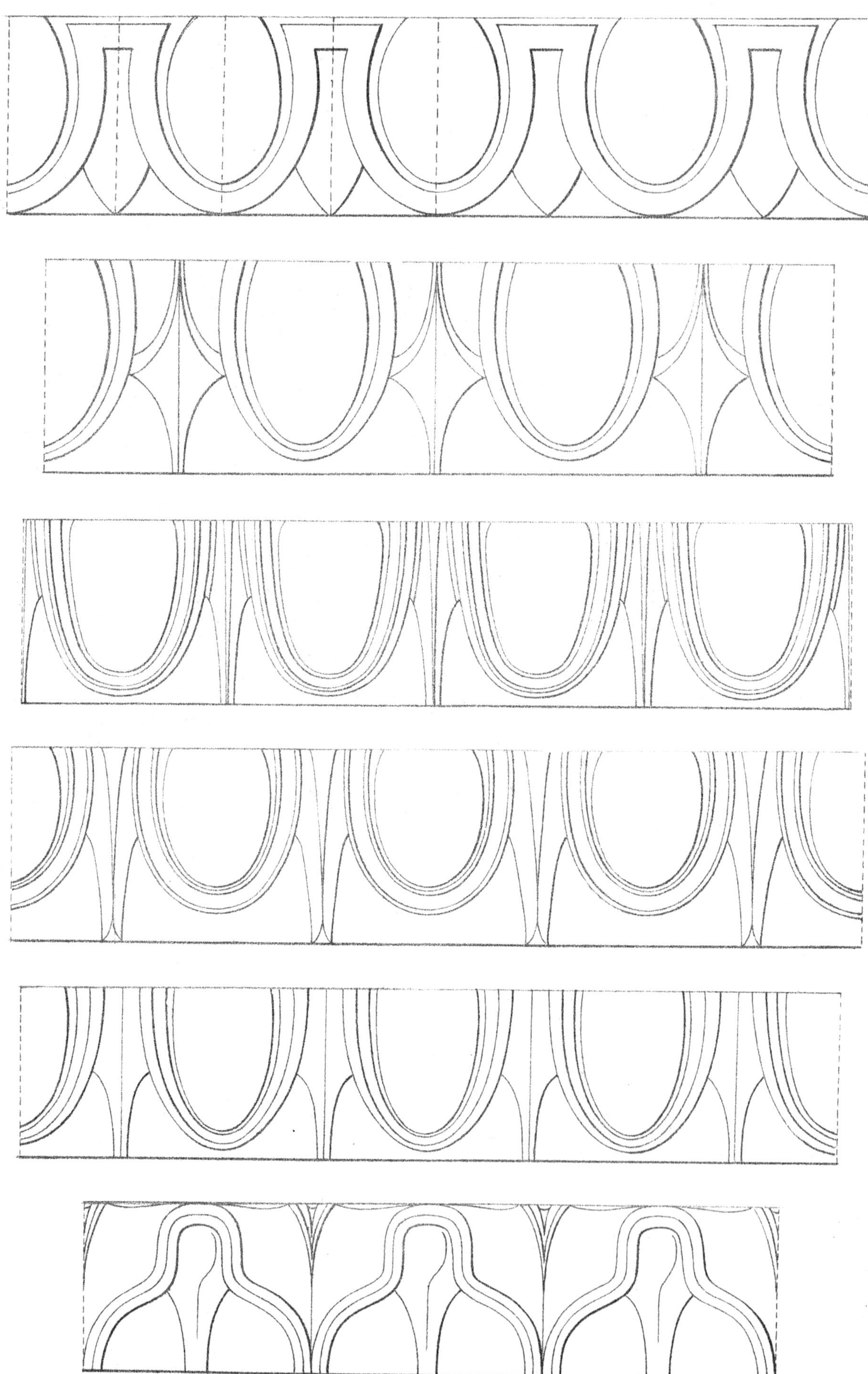

Plate 6

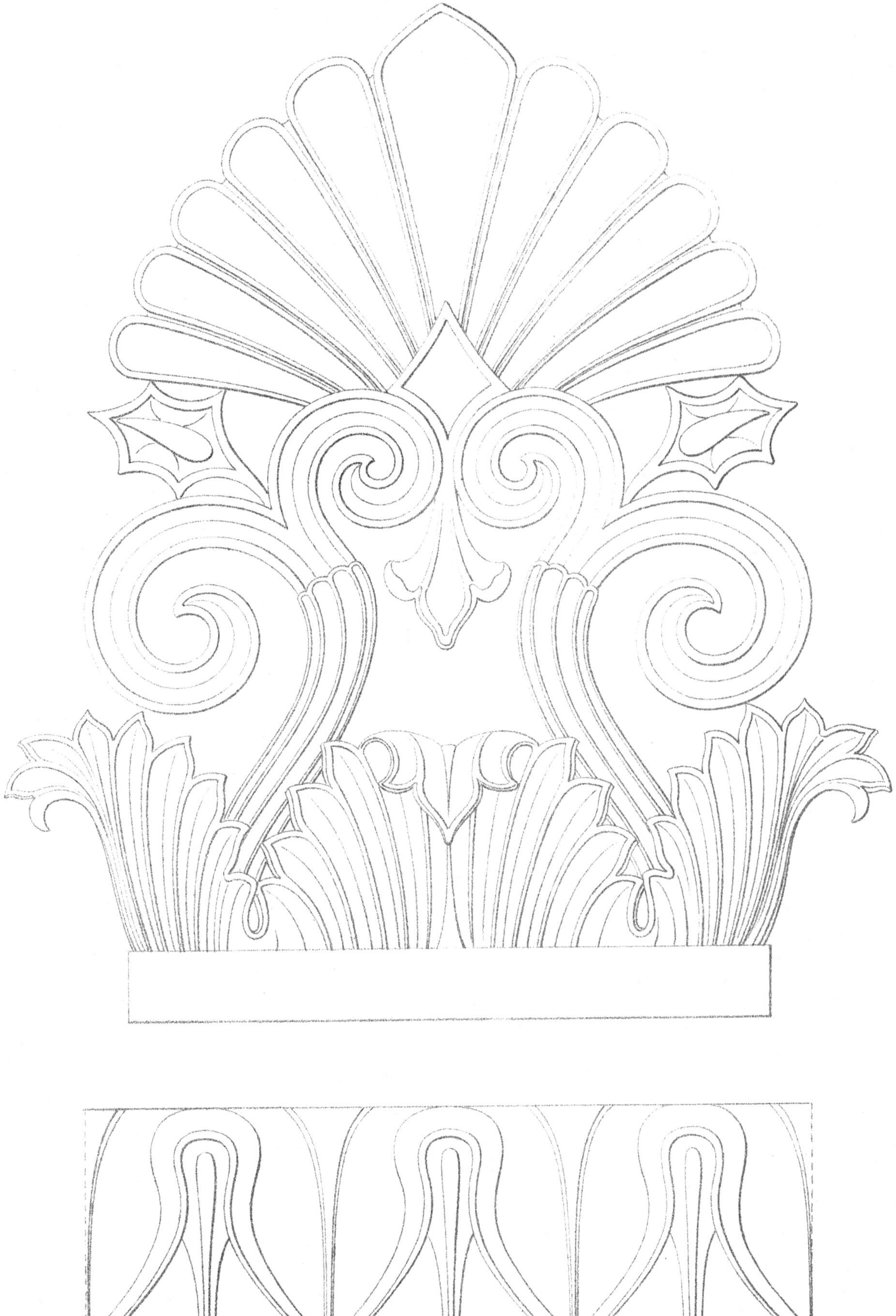

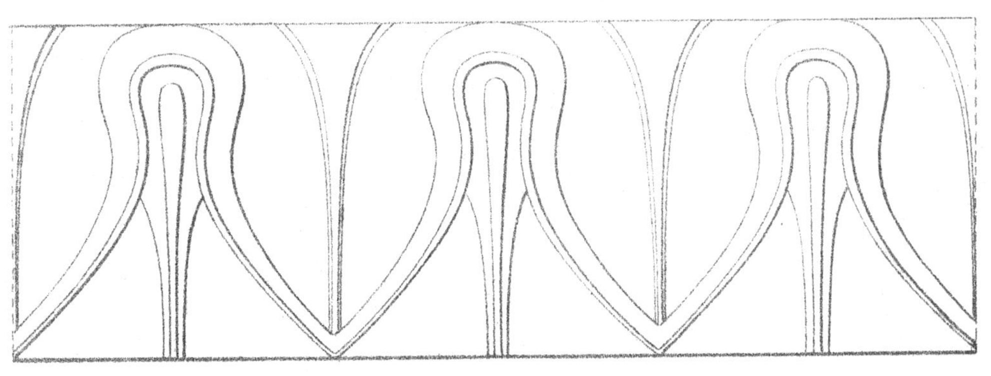

Cap of a gravestone in marble
(Preserved on the Acropolis in Athens)

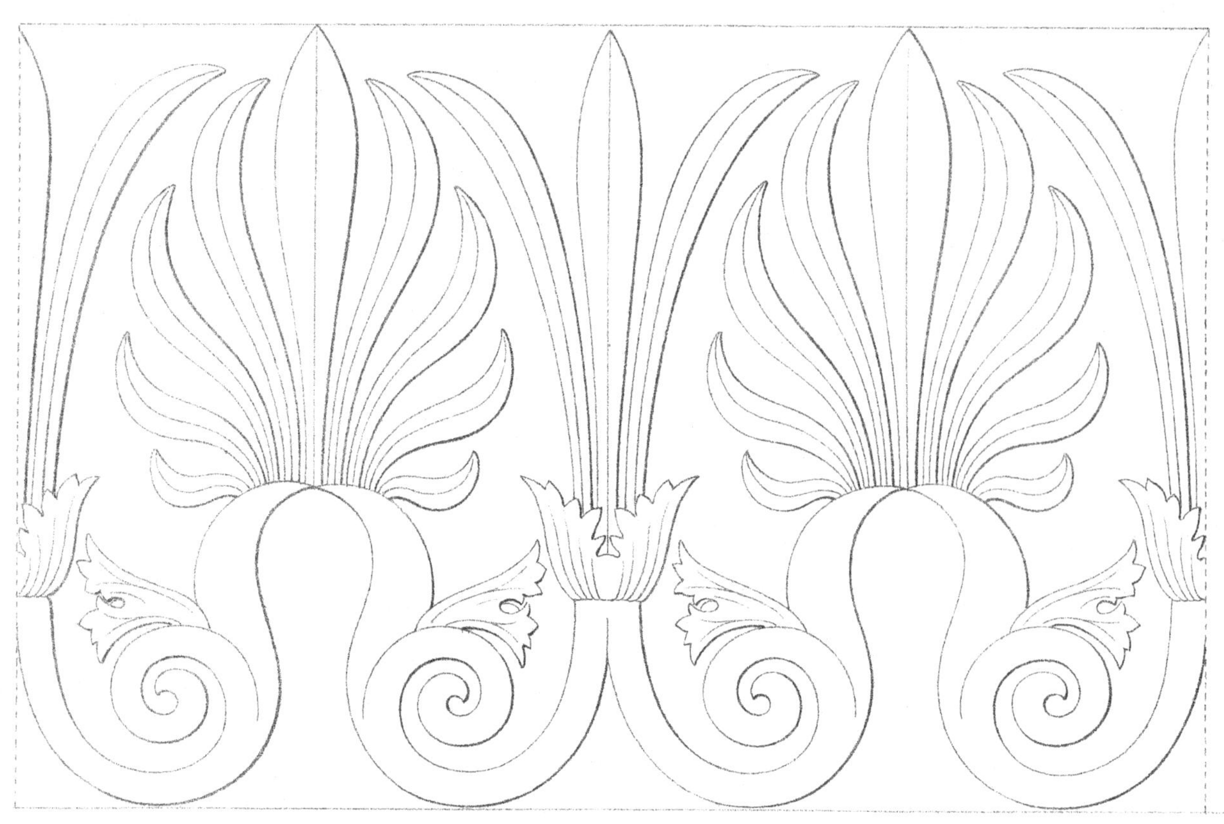

Villa Albani in Rome

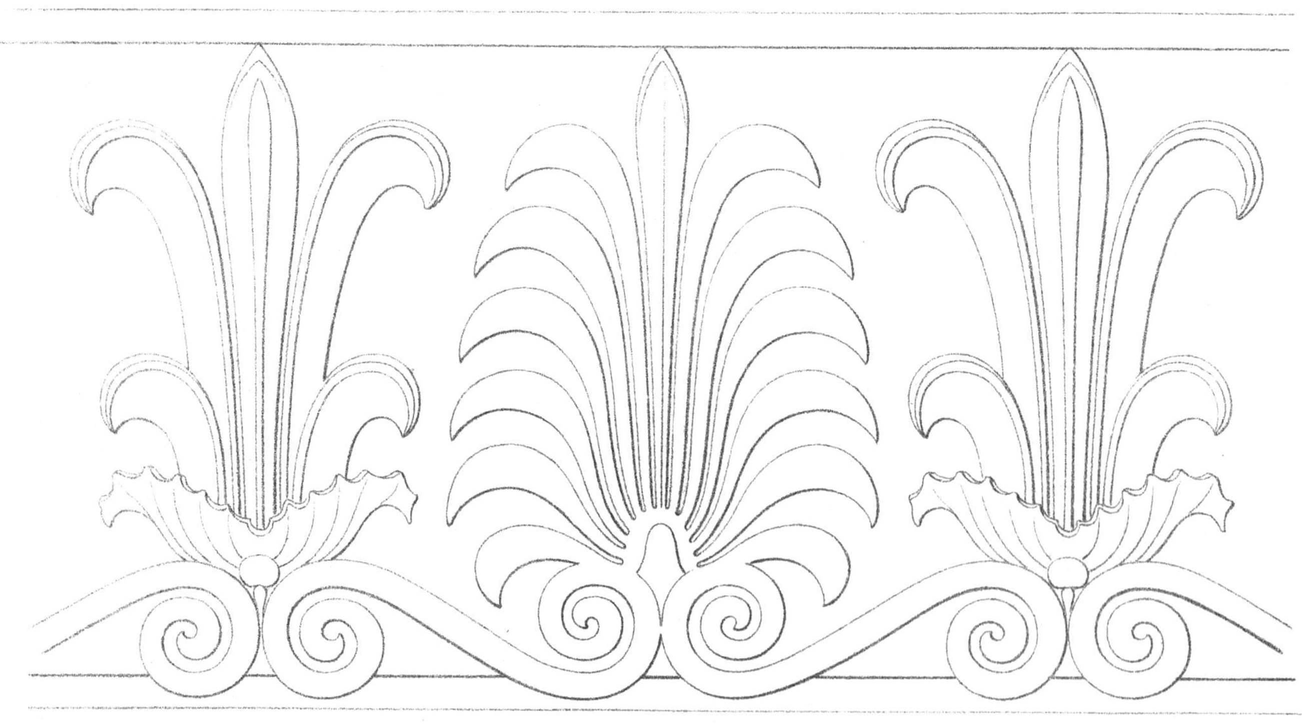

Carnic decoration on the main cornice of the temple of Apollo in Bassae (at Phigalia)

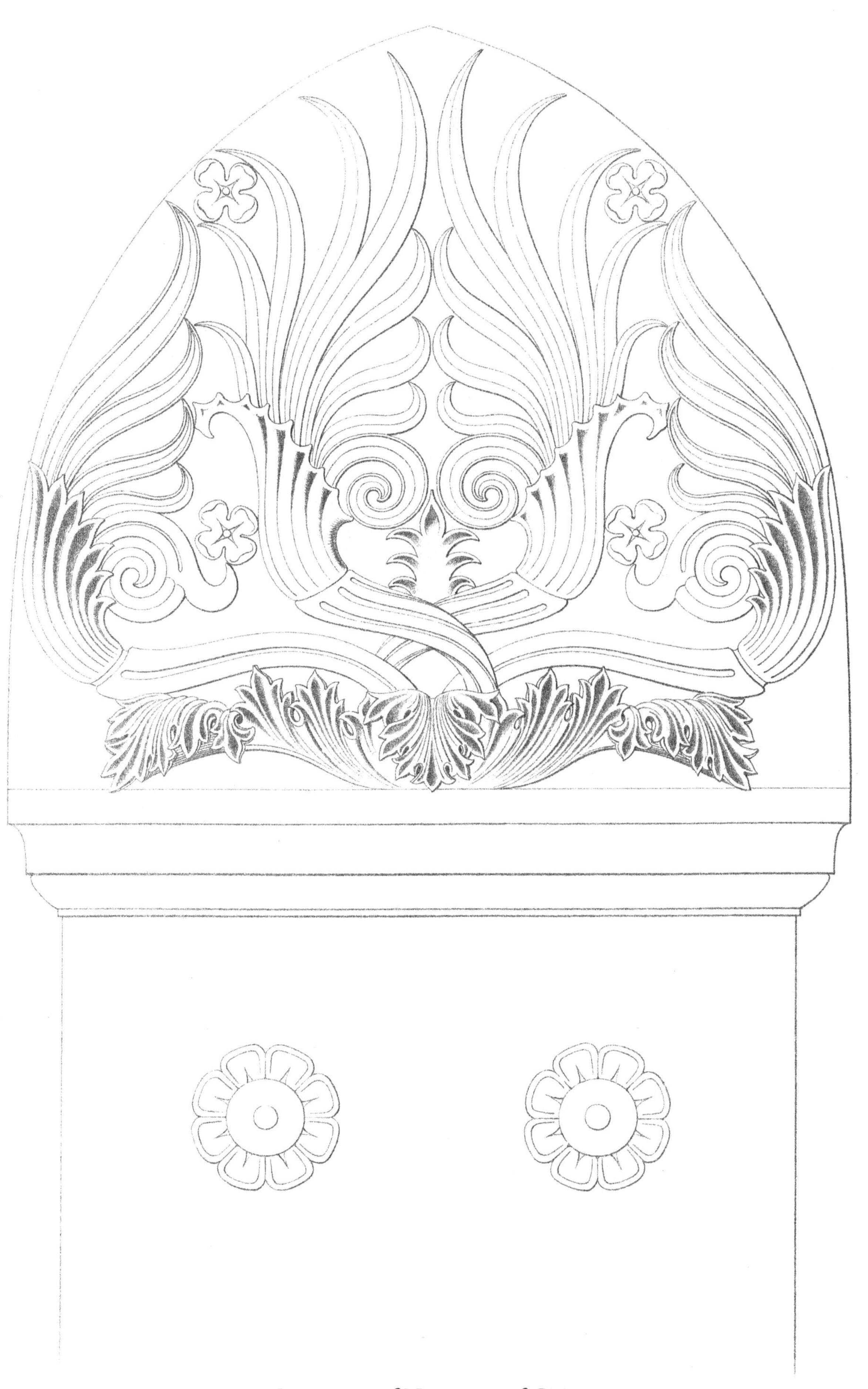

Gravestone of Numenius of Citium

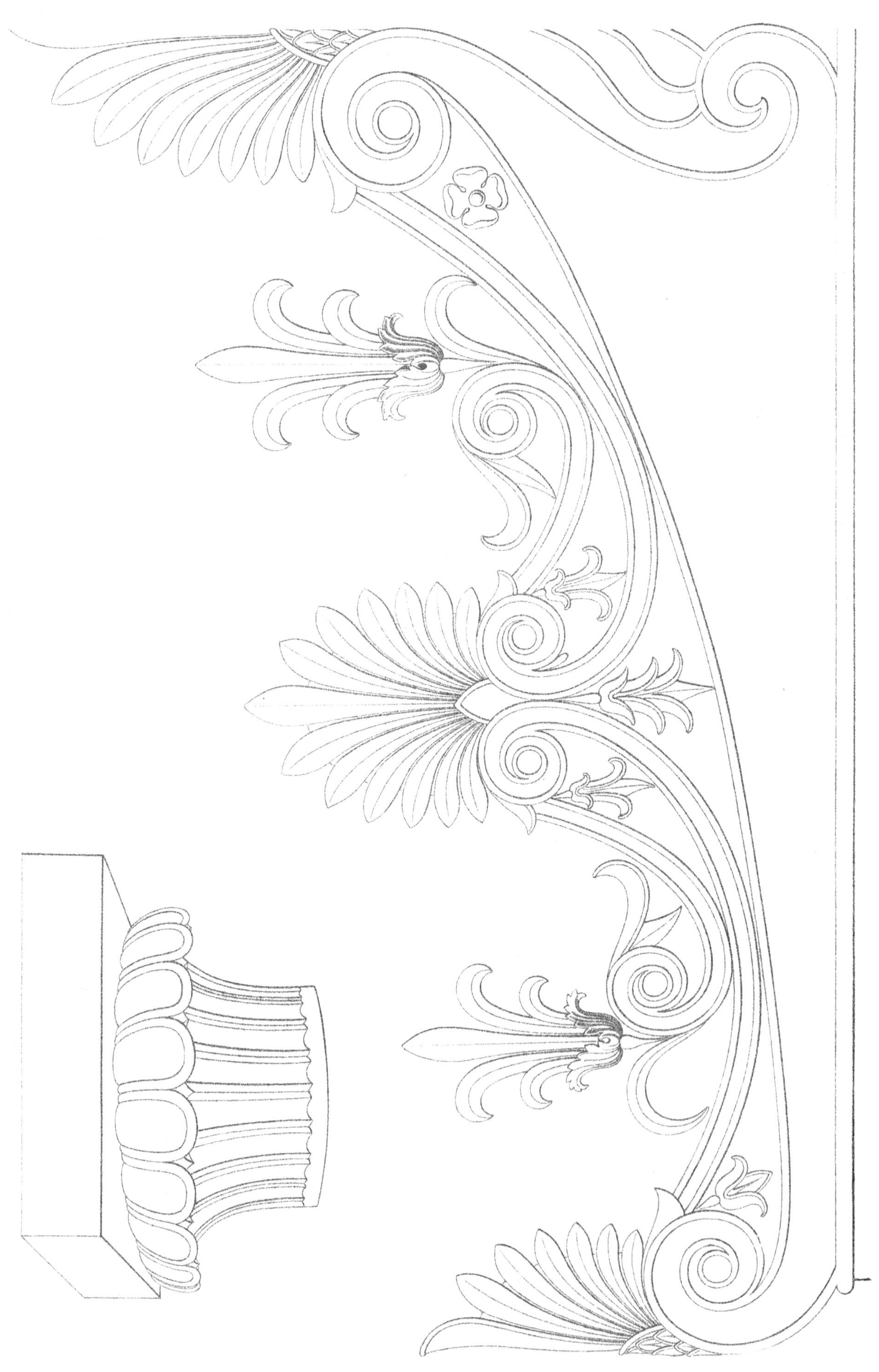

Made of white marble near Epidaurus

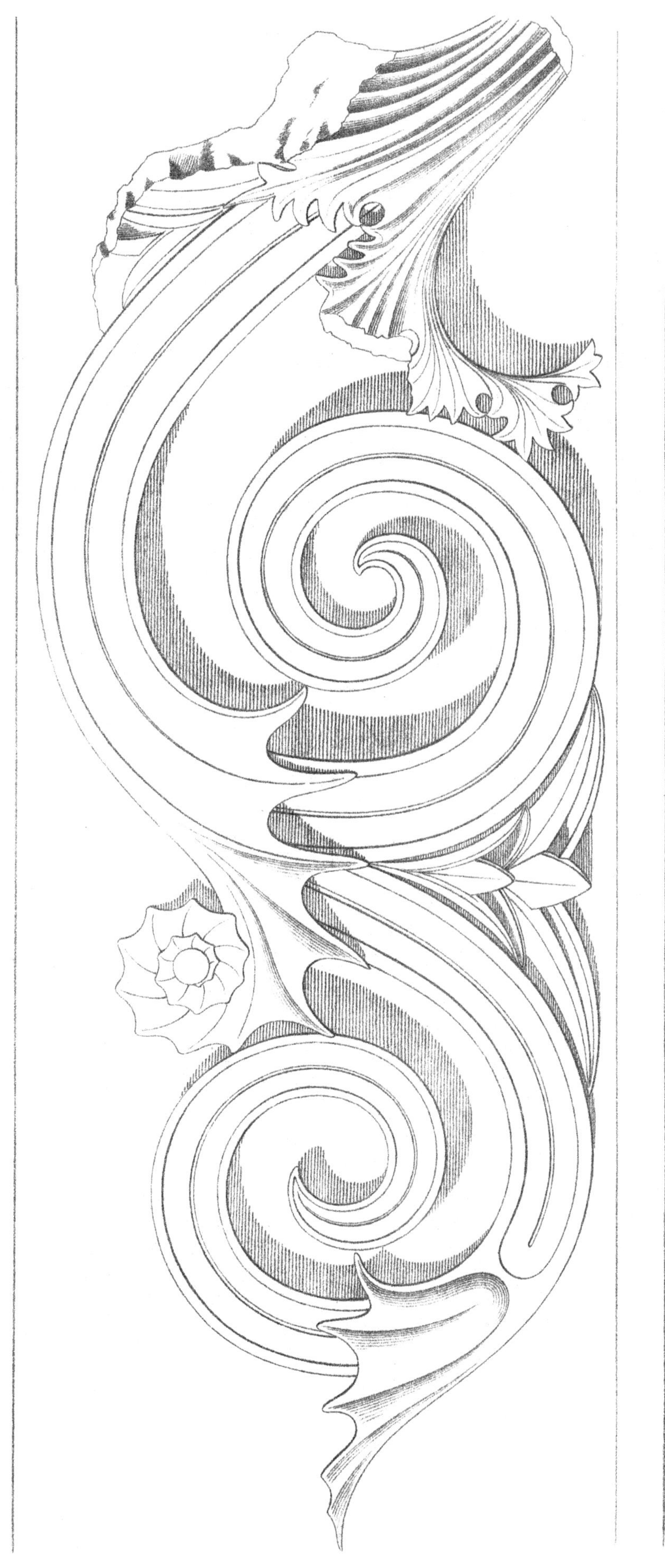

From a monument of Lysicrates of Athens

Painted decoration in the Ionic temple of Illisus in Athens

Frieze from the ruins of a temple at Magnesia

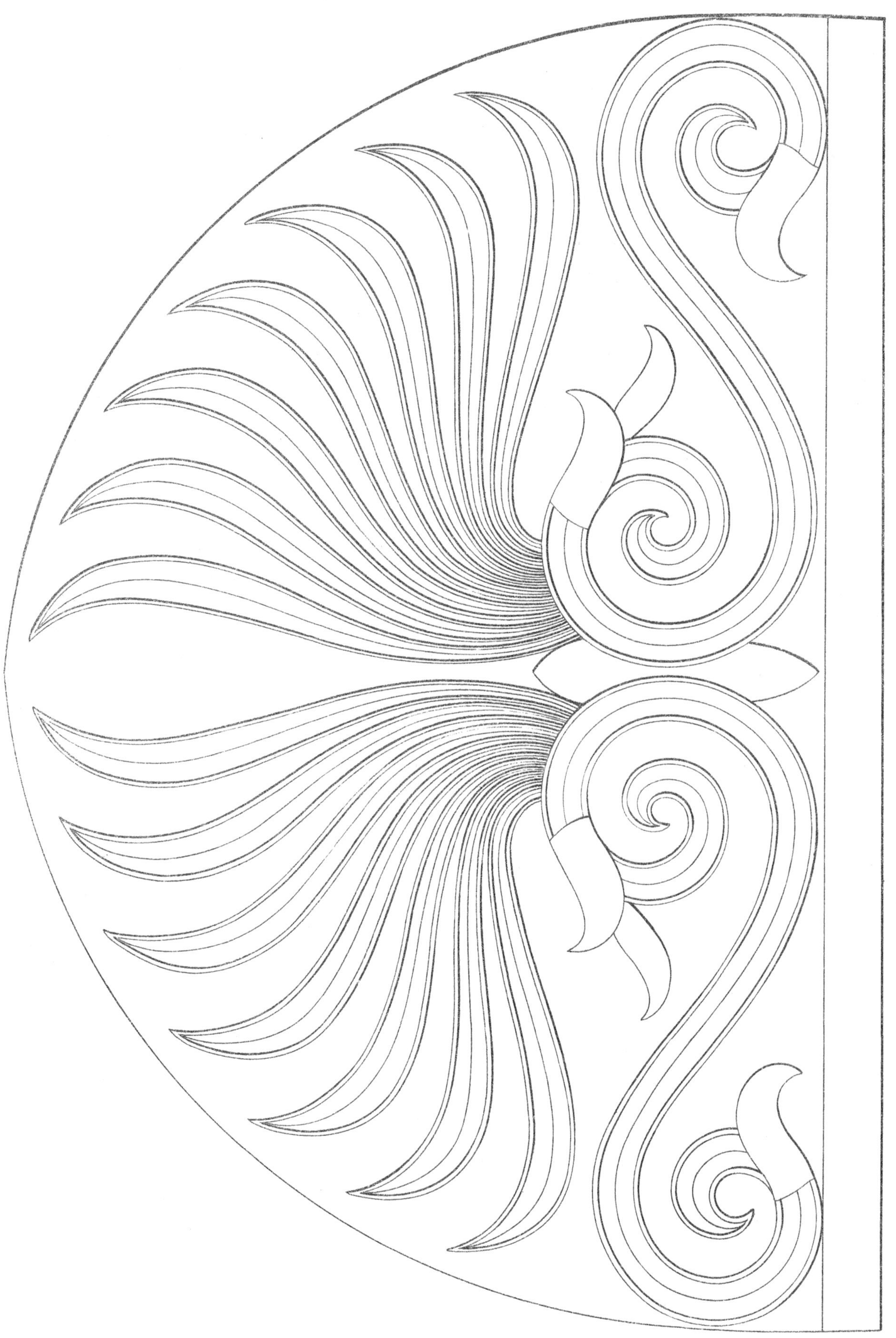

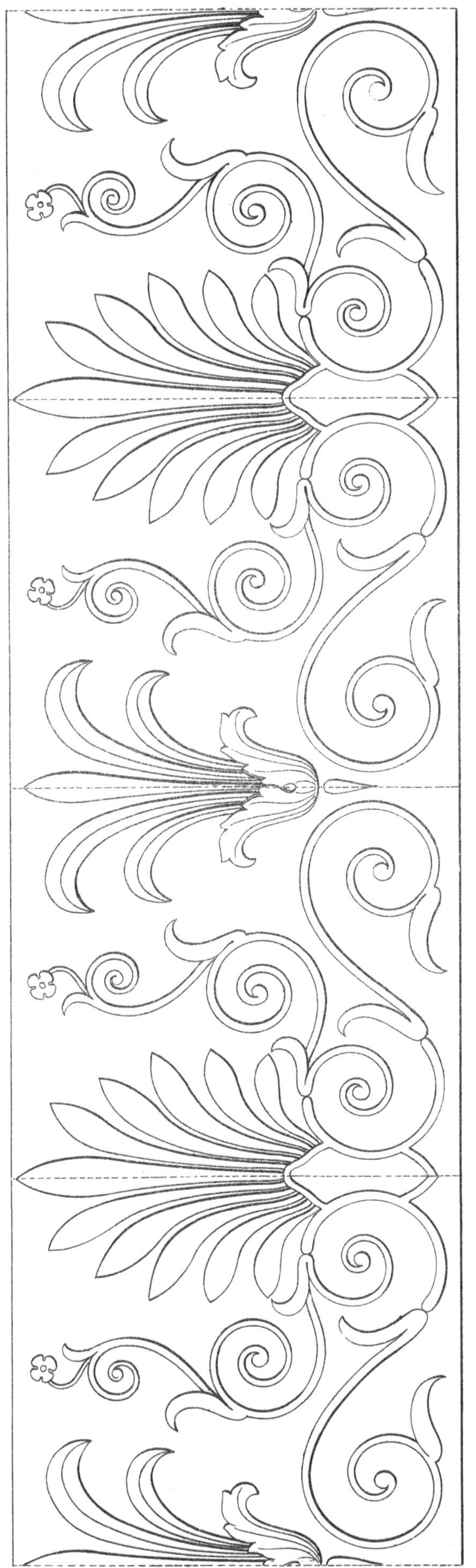

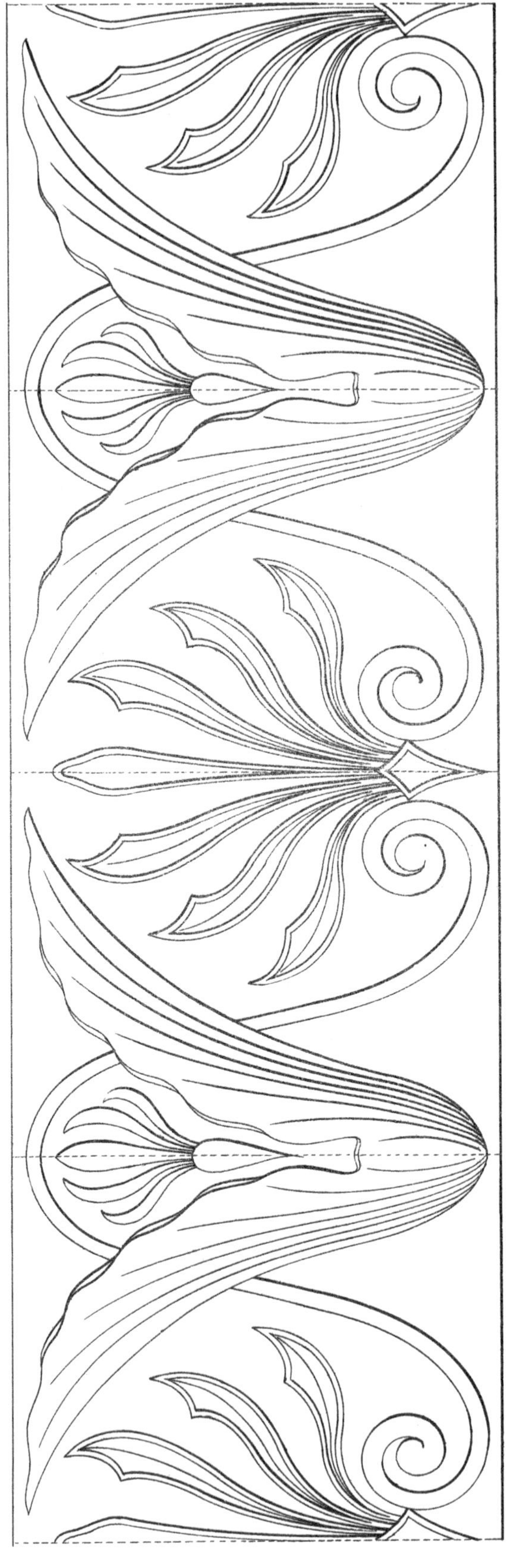

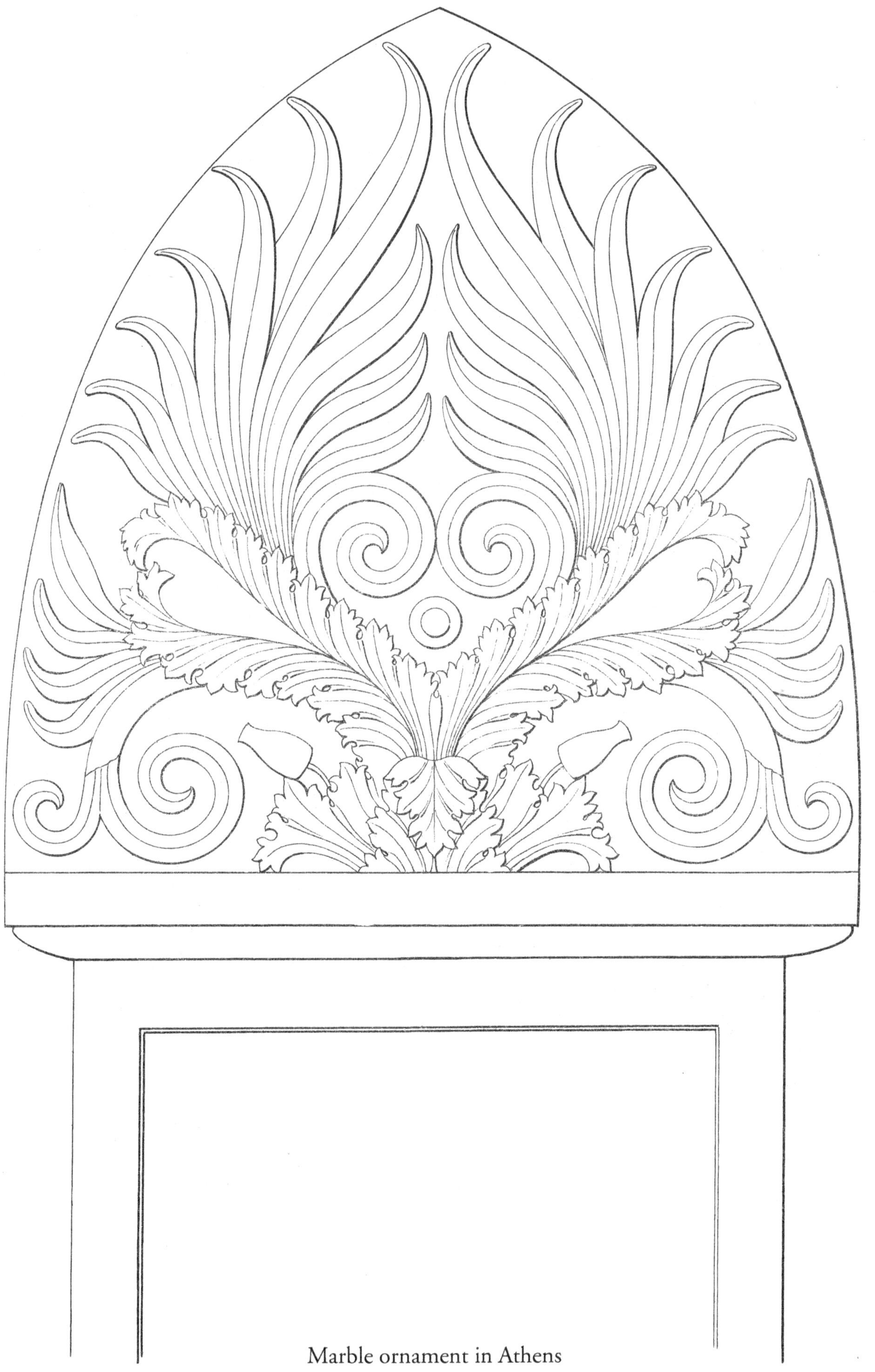

Marble ornament in Athens

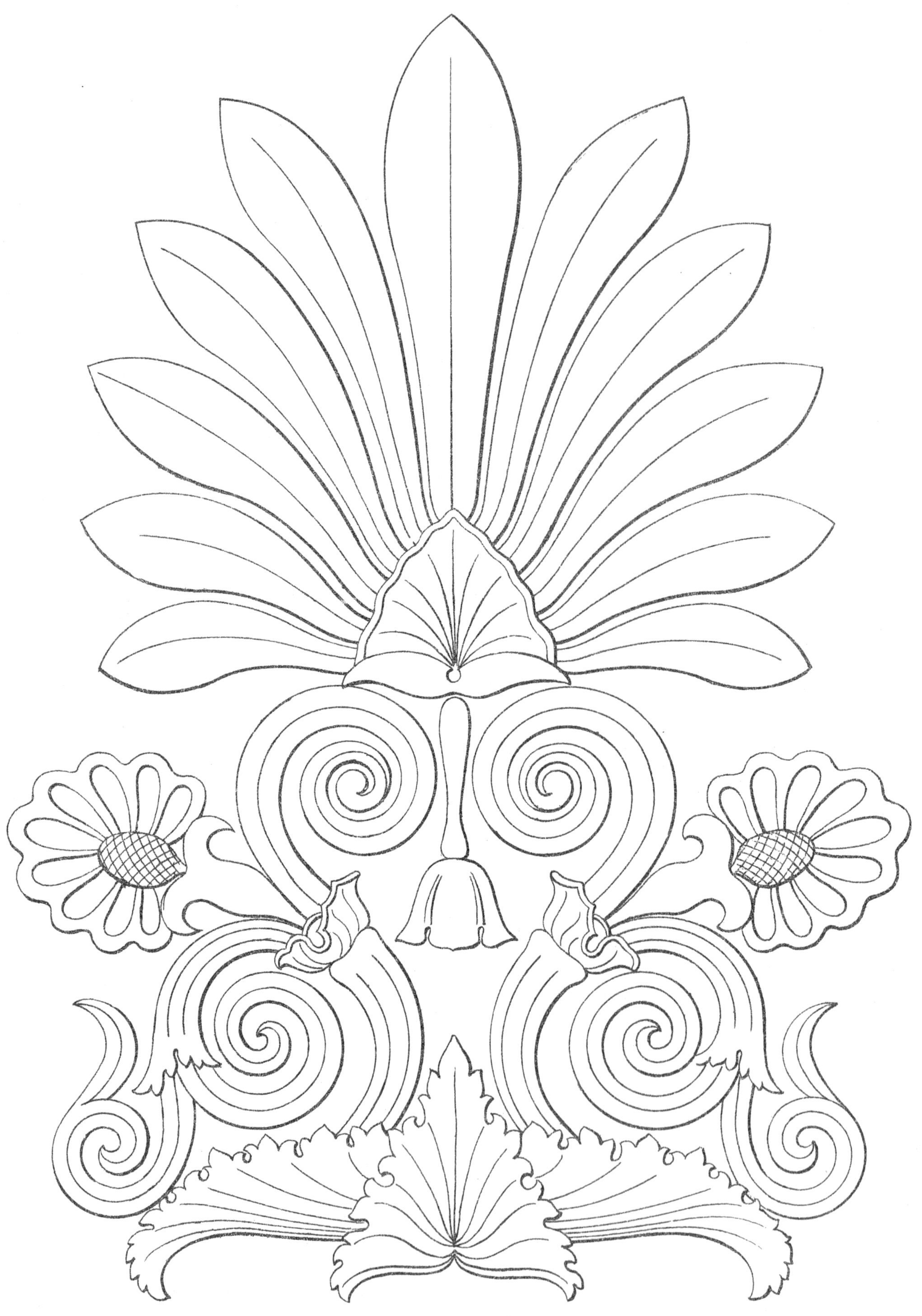

Ornament in Athens

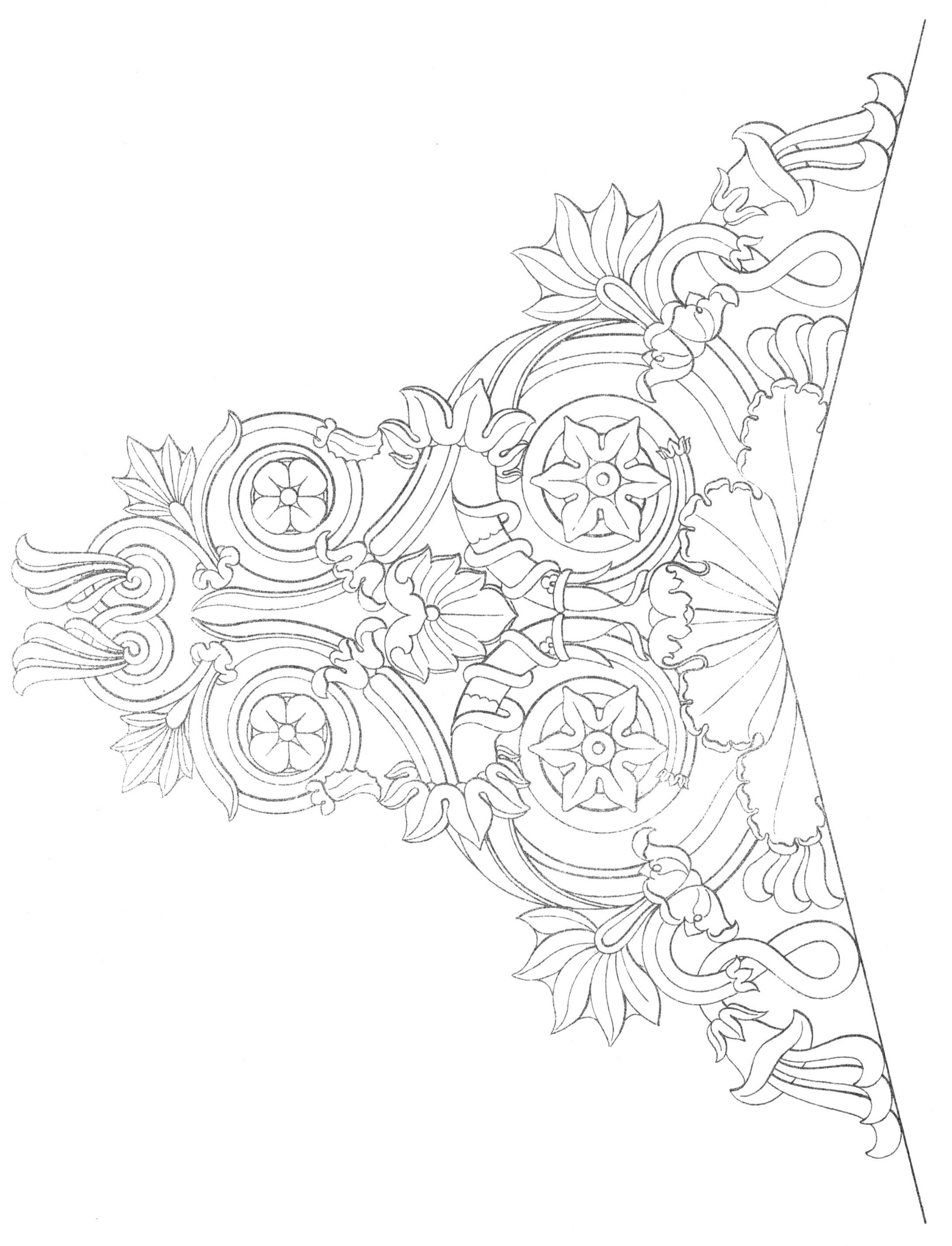

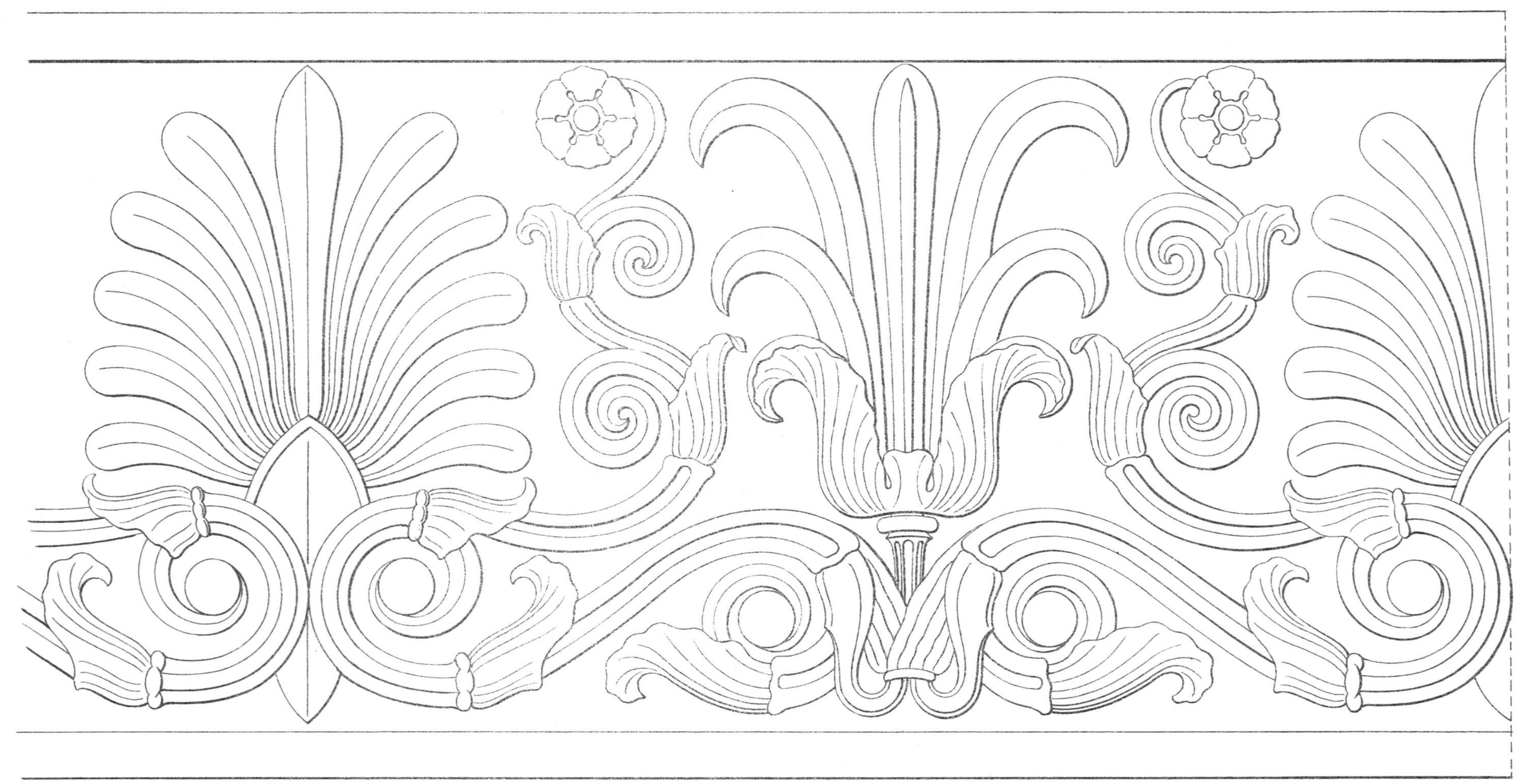

Frieze on the temple of Minerva in Athens

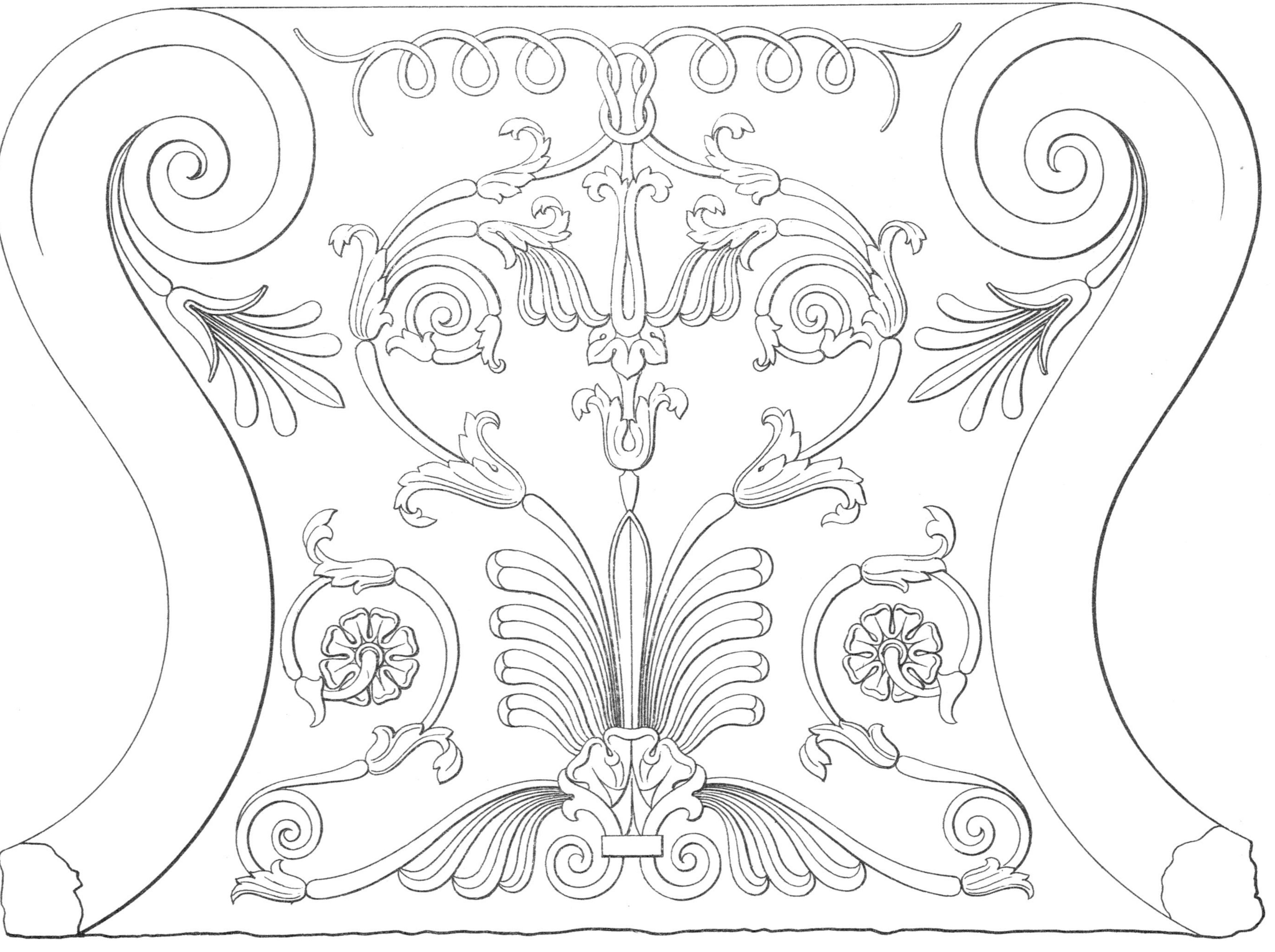

Ornament on an antique white marble armchair in Rome
(In the church of St. Stephan)

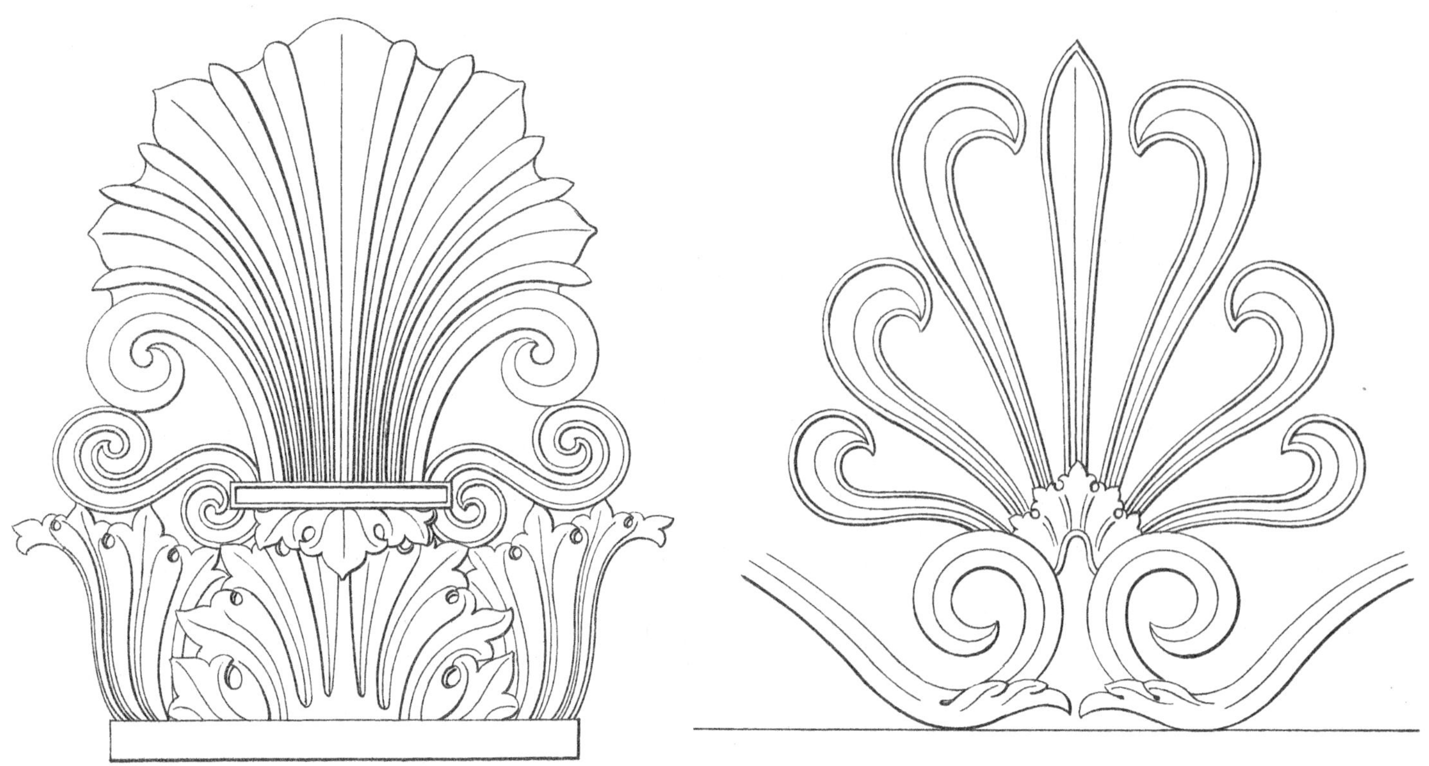

From Pompeii

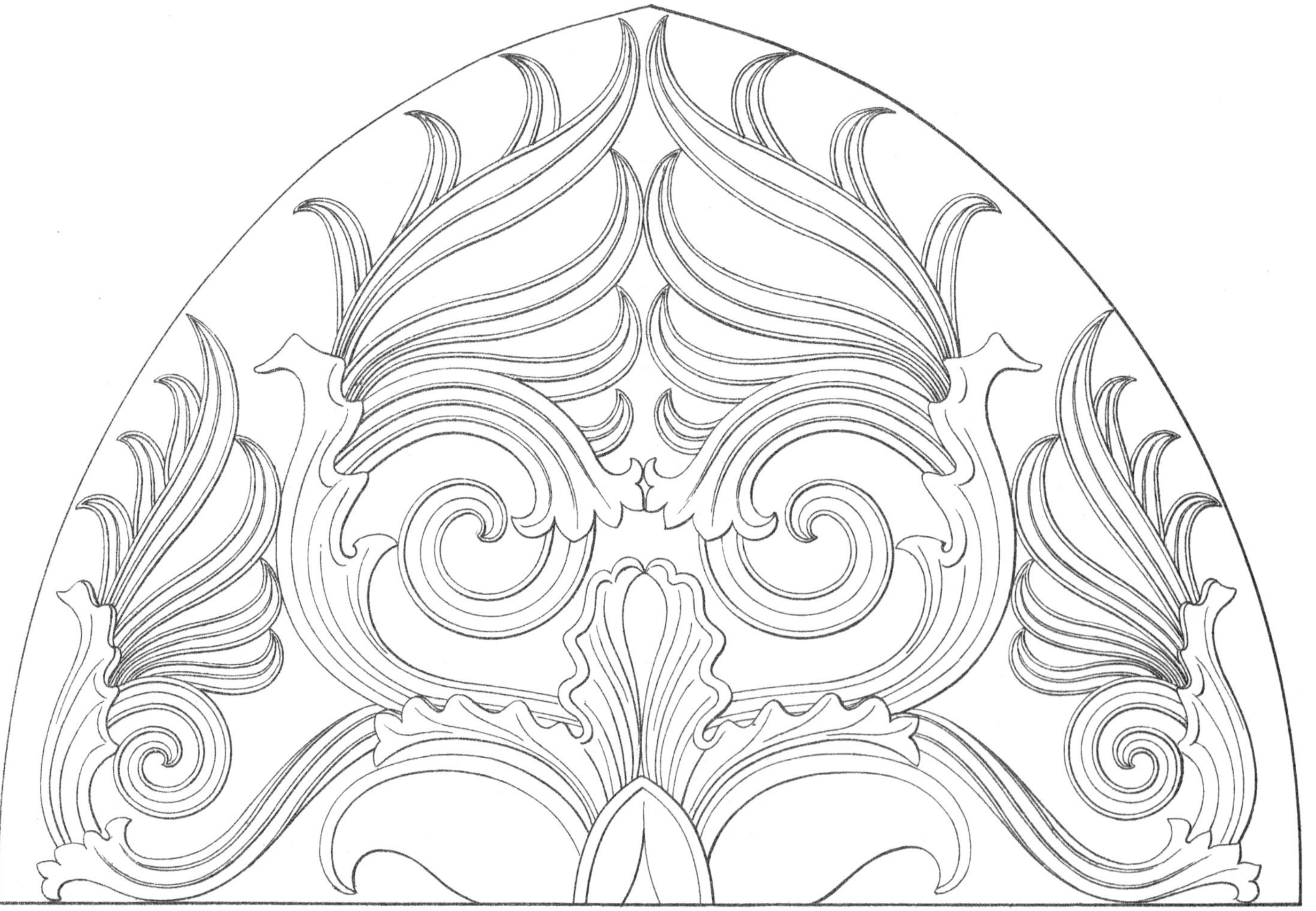

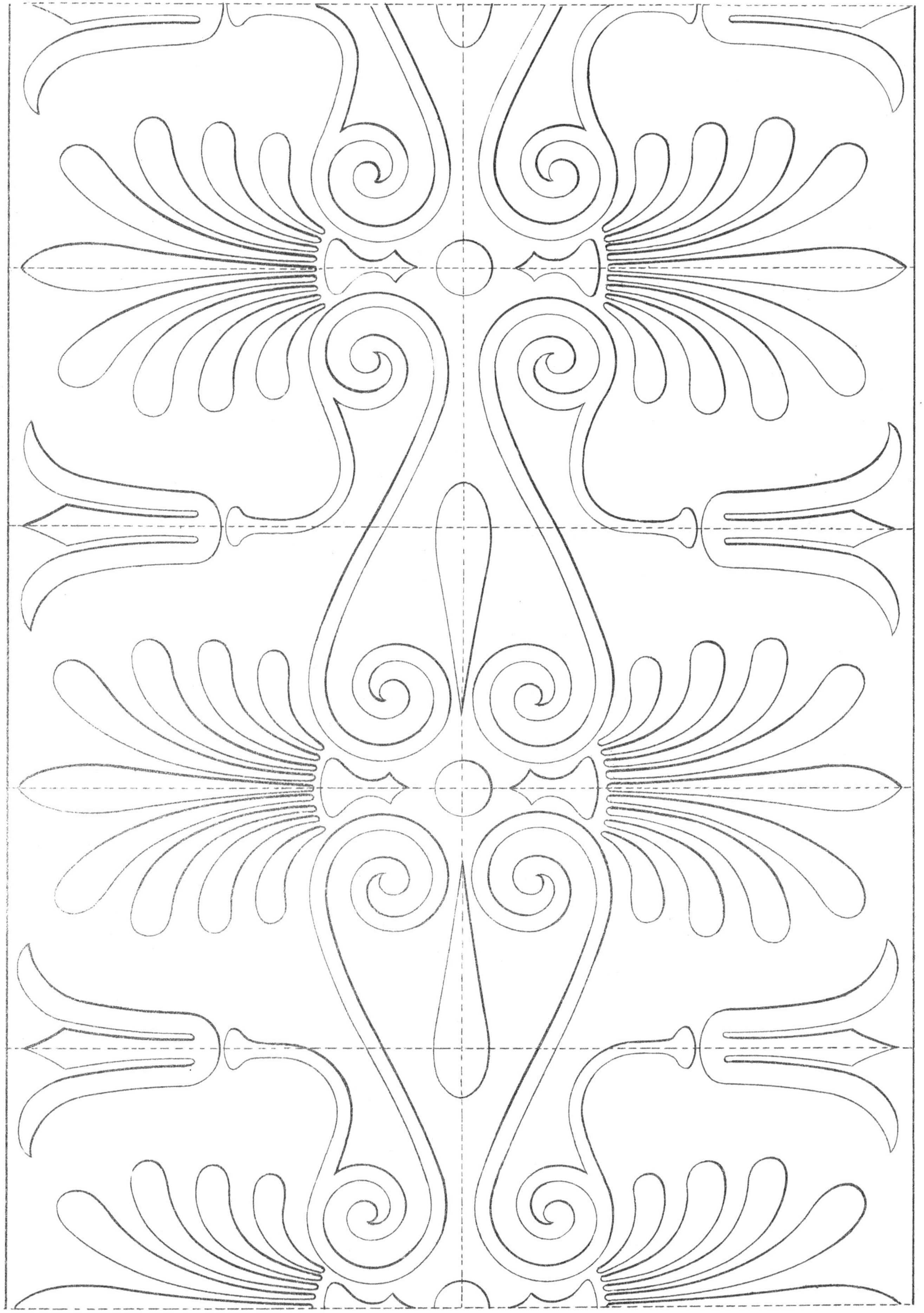

Plate 21

Cap of an antique gravestone made of marble

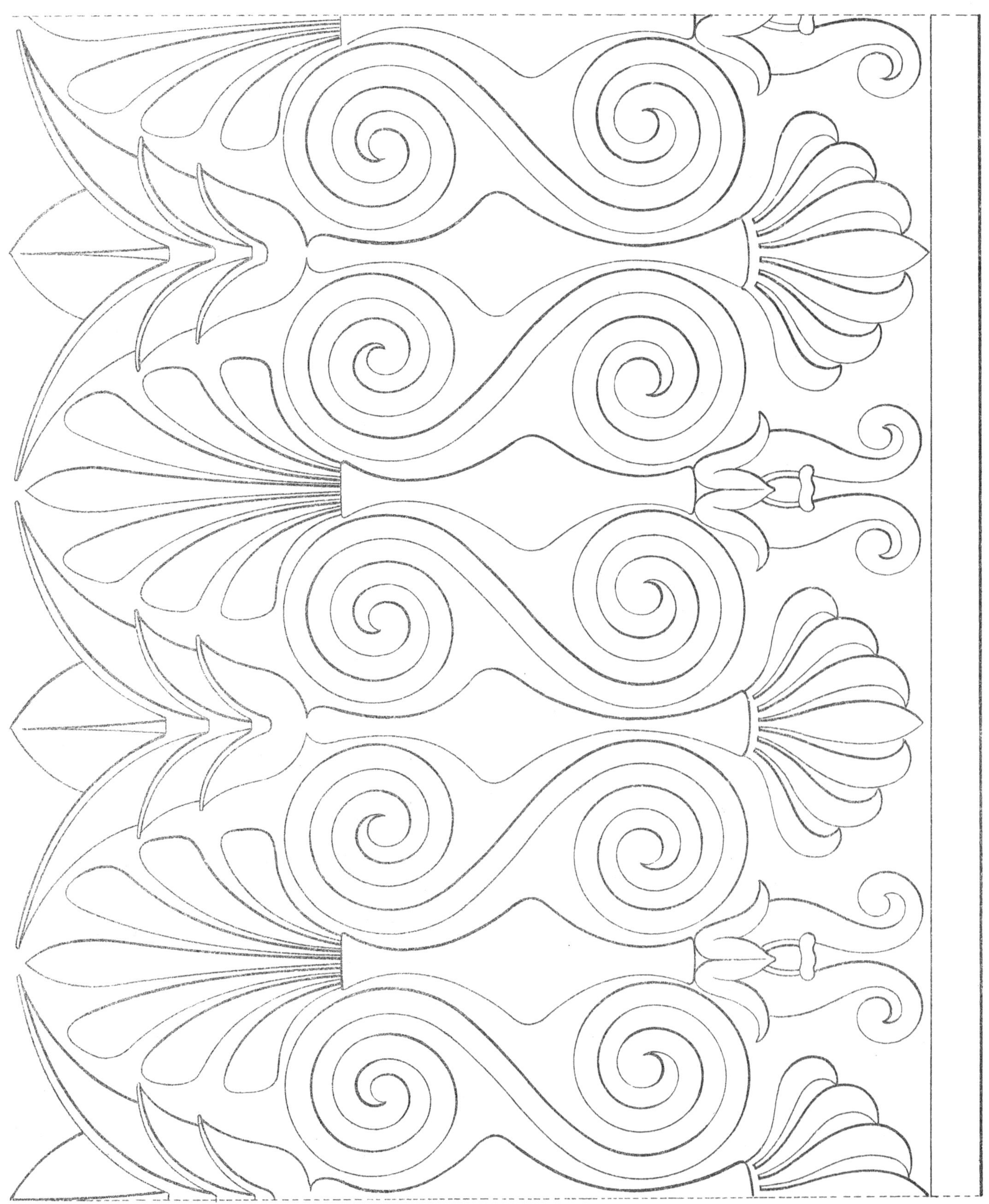

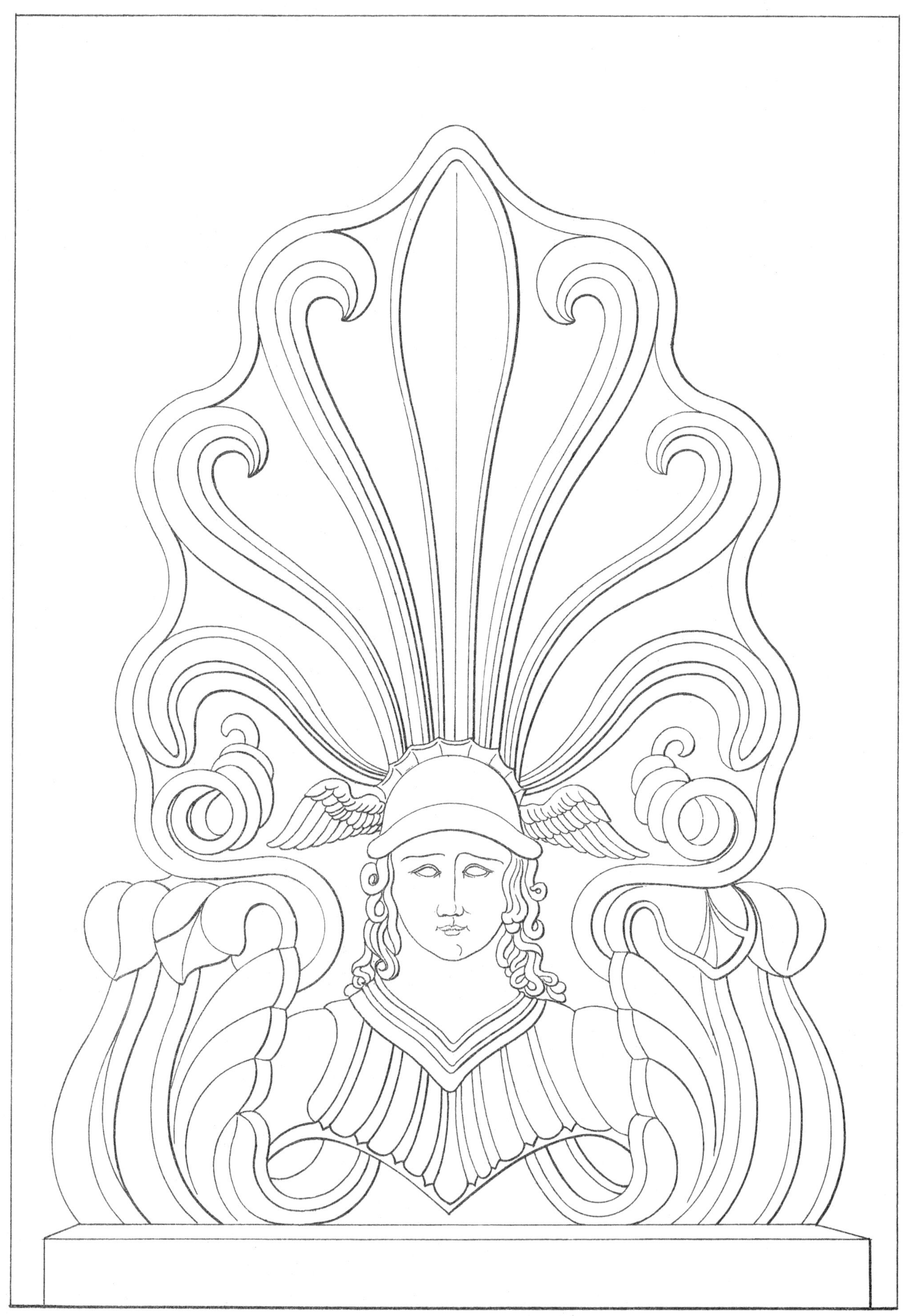

Plate 24

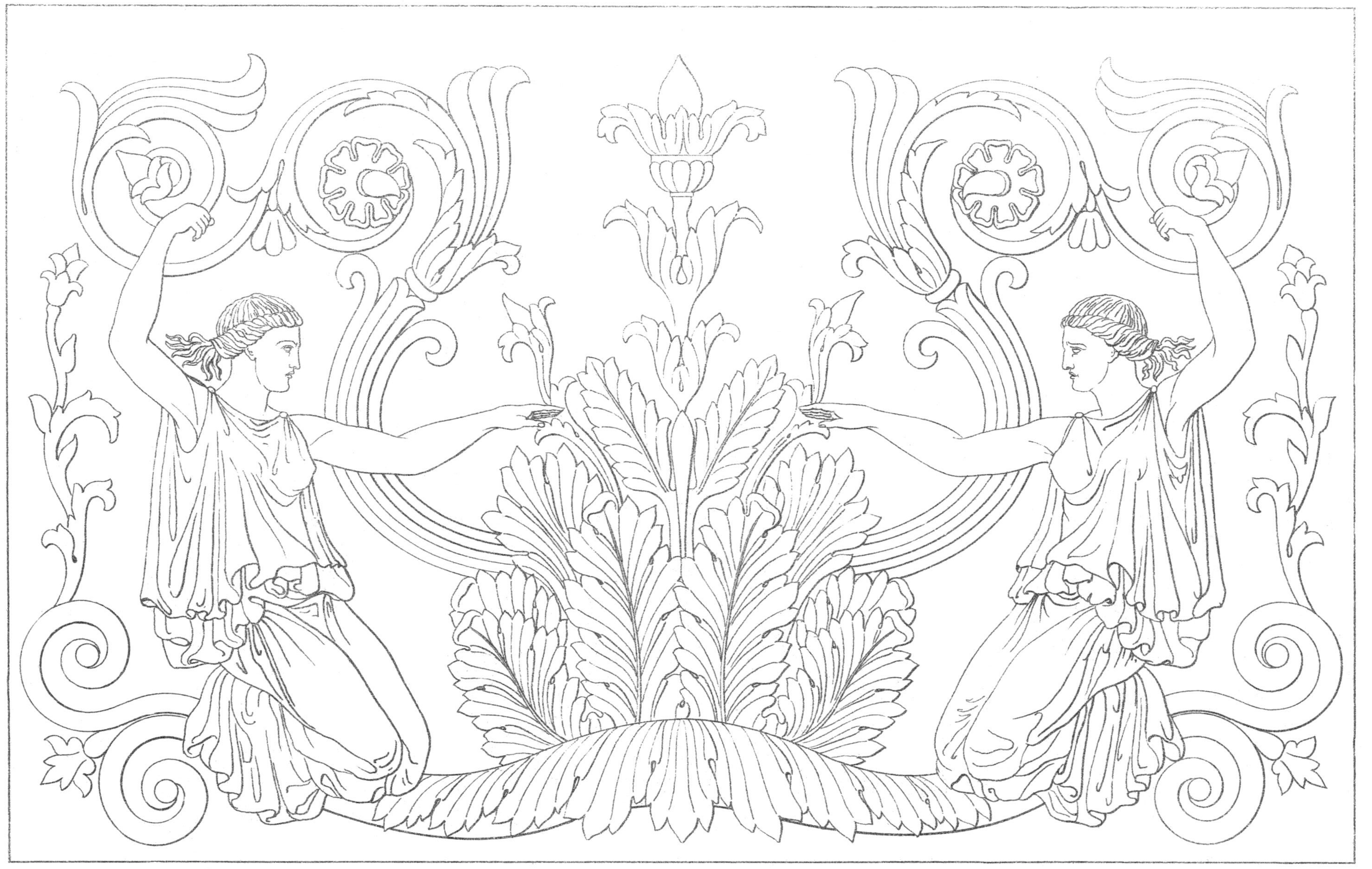

From the Vatican Museum

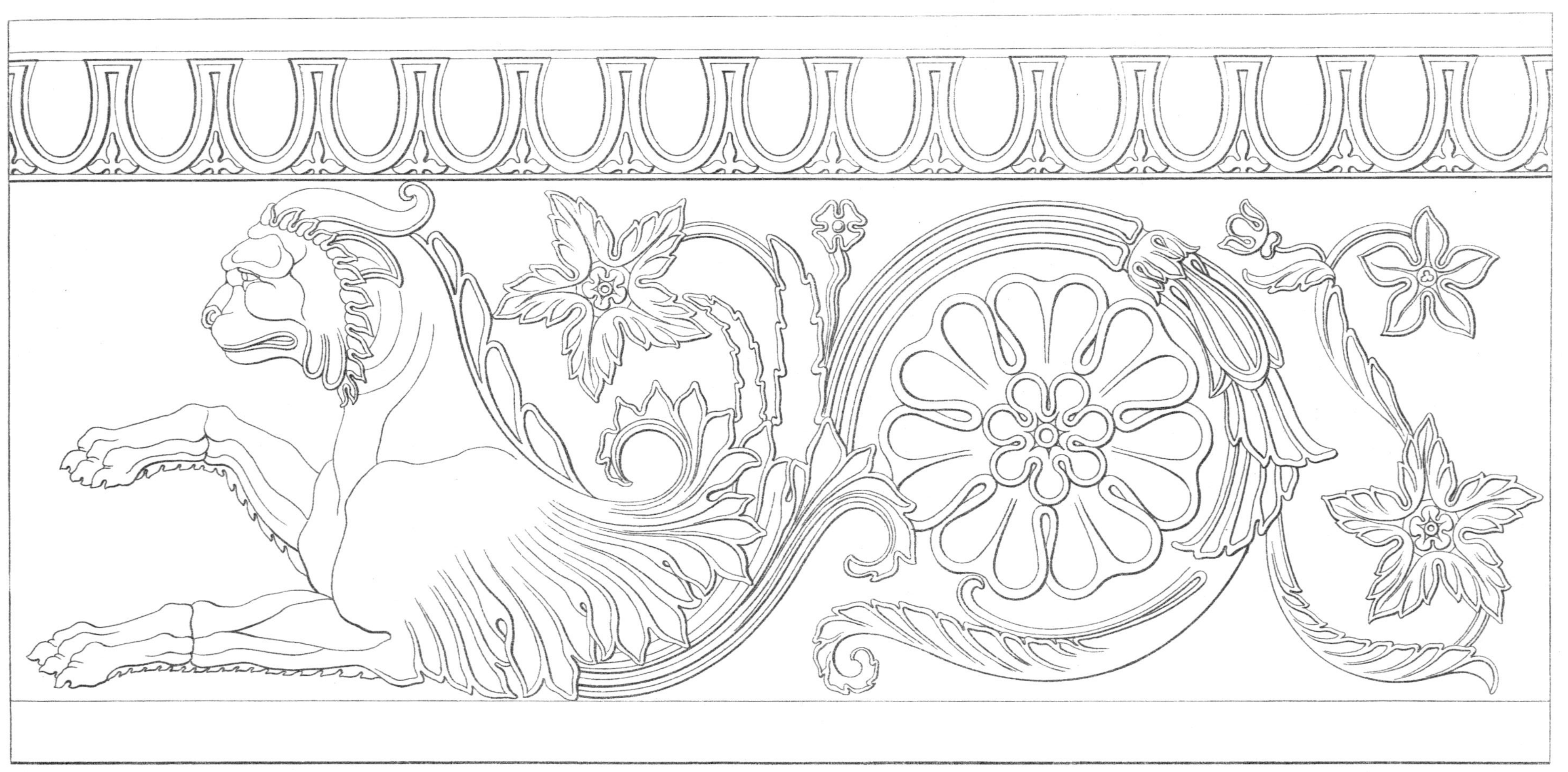

From the Kircherian Museum

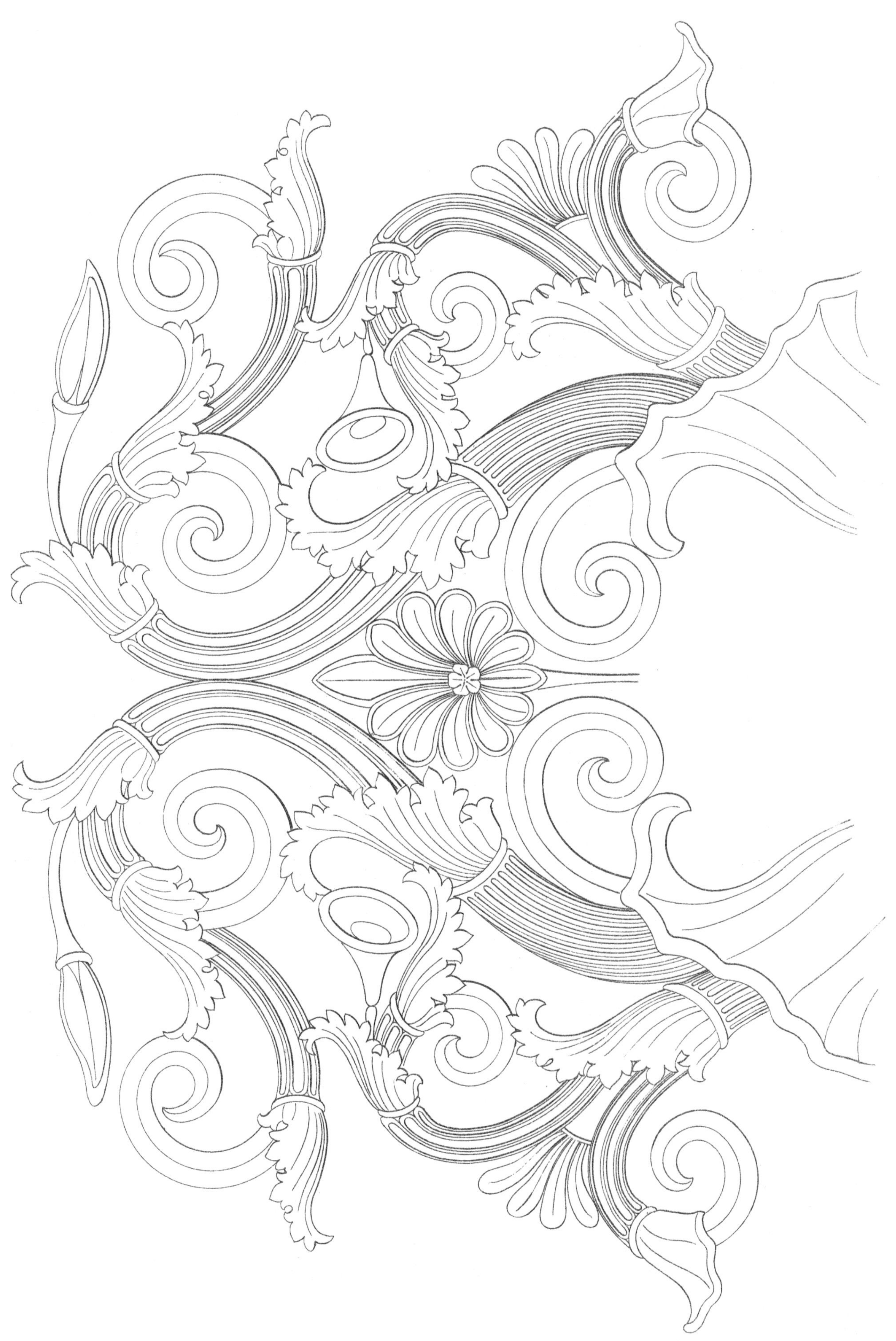

Plate 28

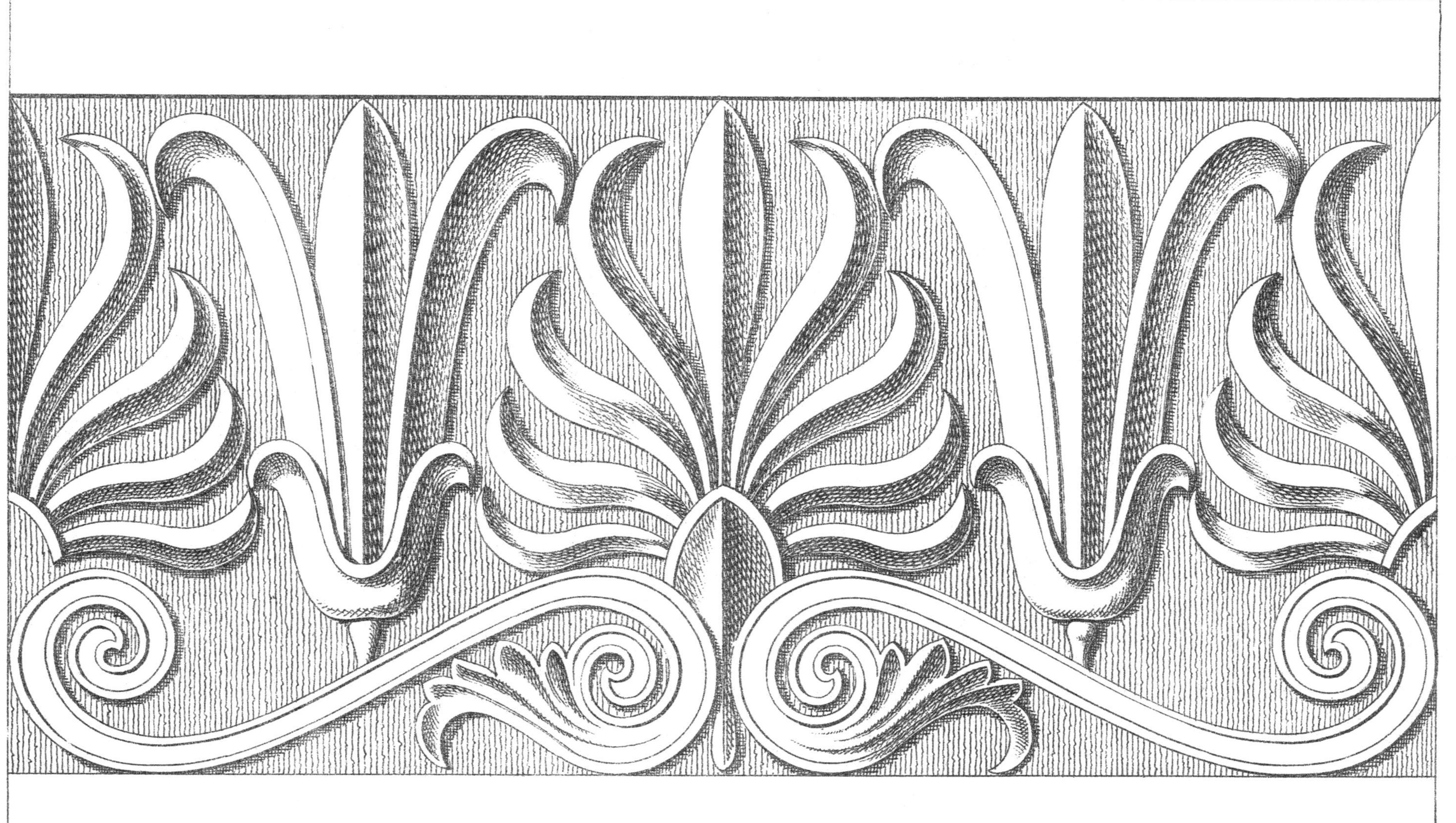

Excavated in Athens in 1838–1839

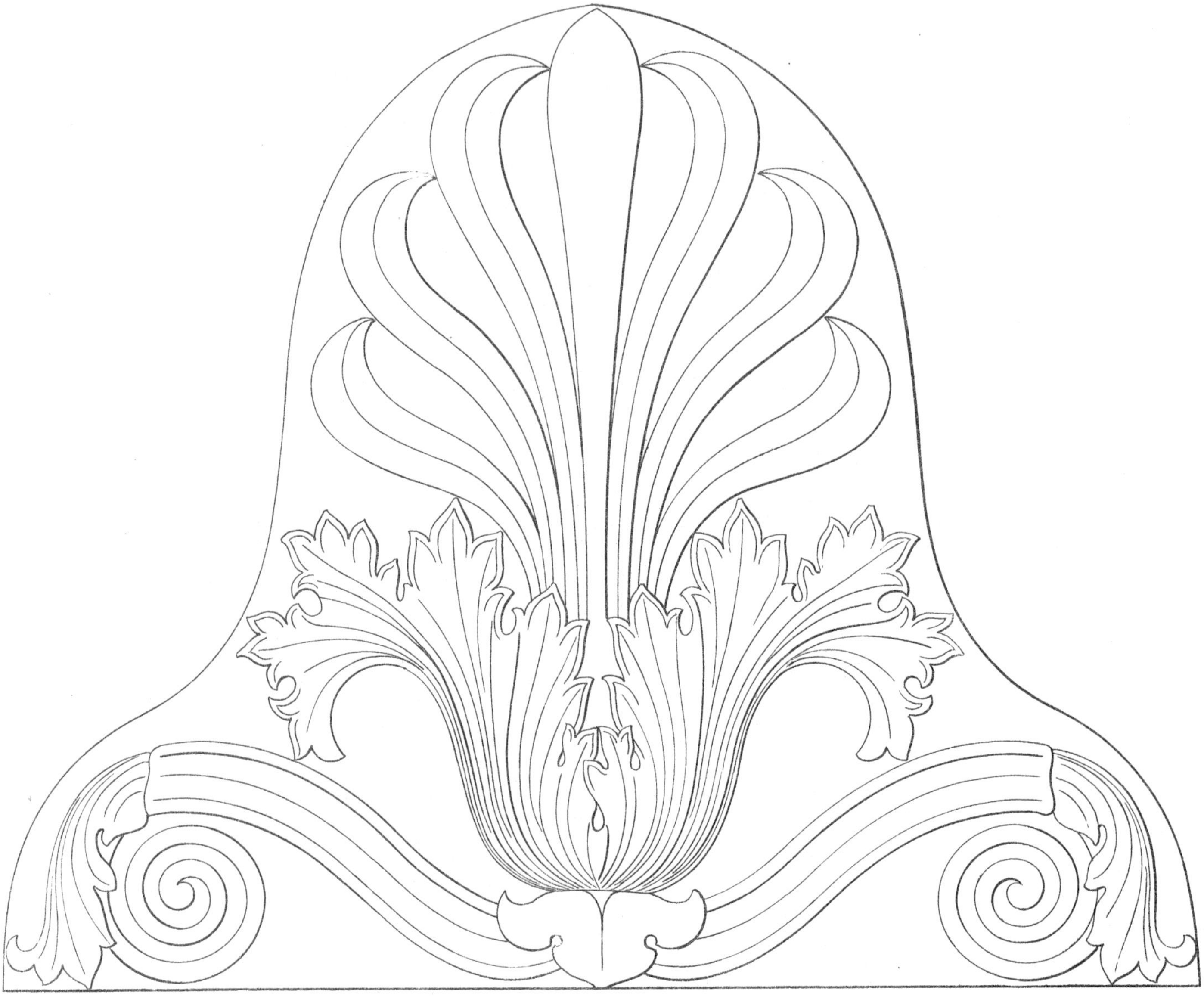

In the temple of Themis at Rhamnus

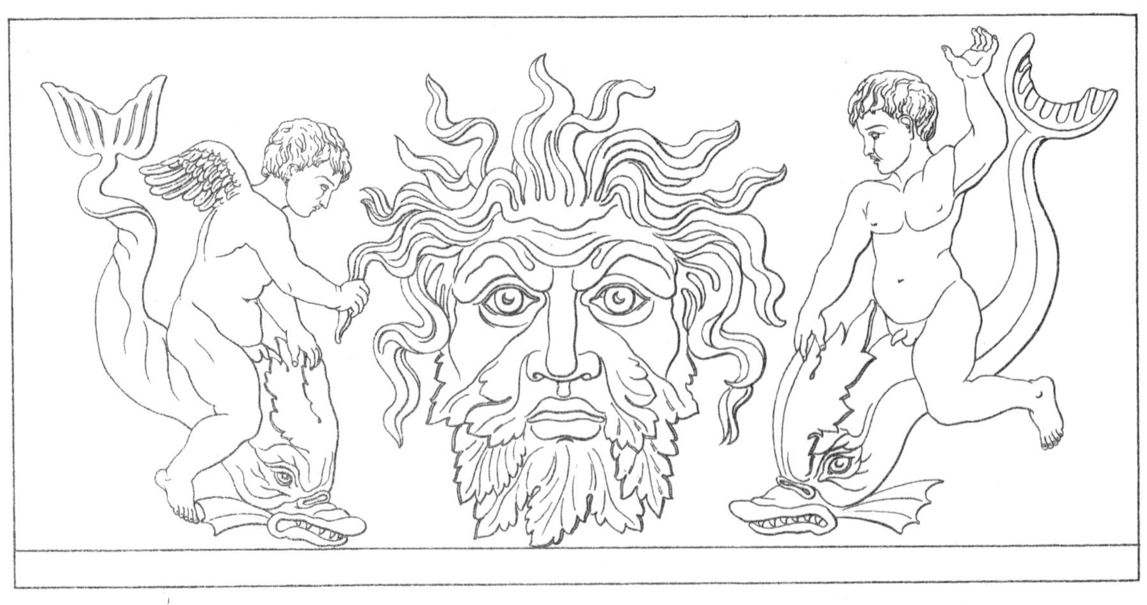

From the British Museum

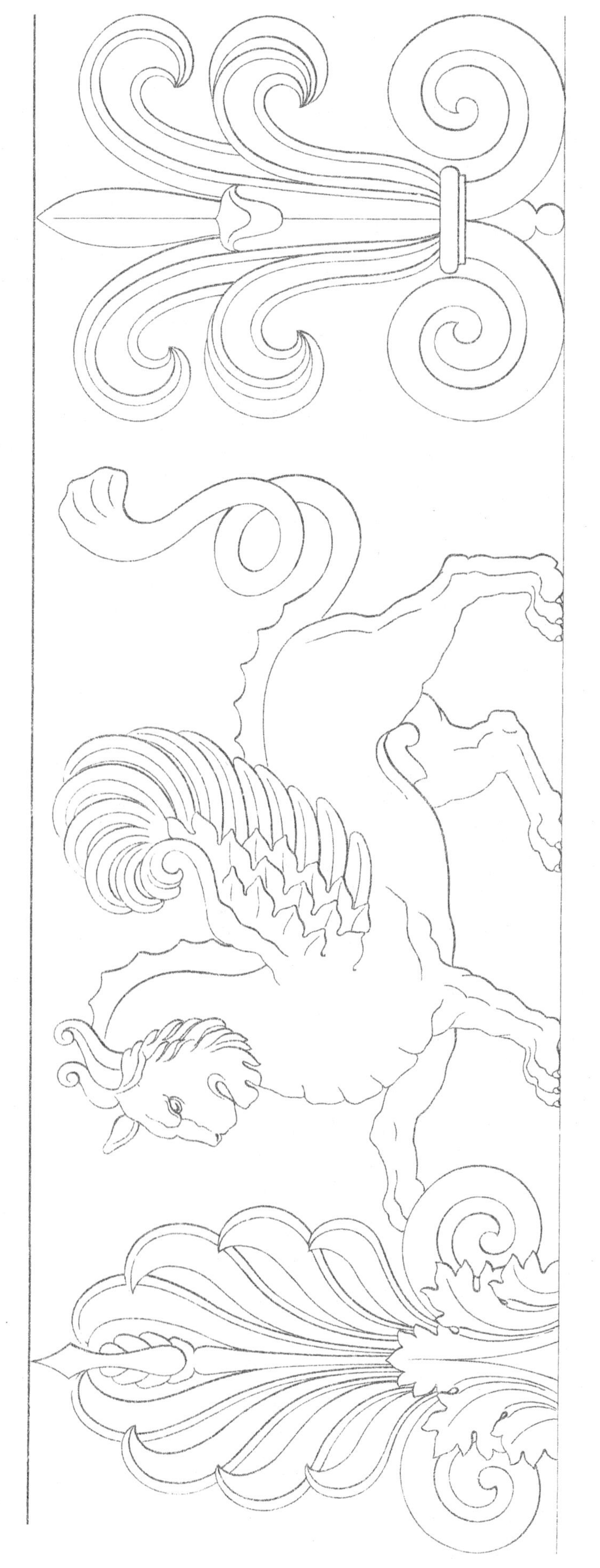

White marble frieze at Pergamus

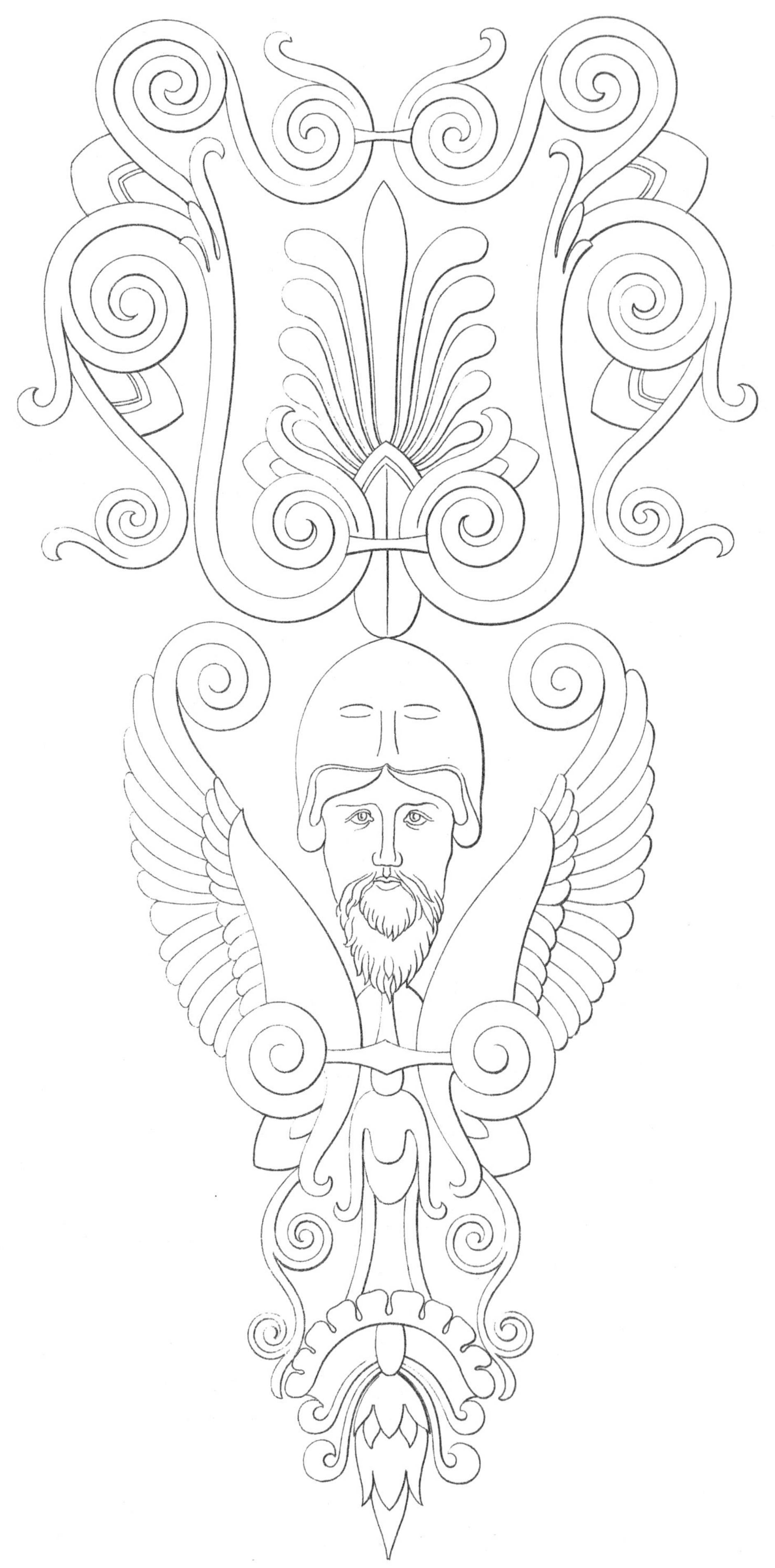

Plate 32

Frieze from the temple of Apollo Didimaeus at Branchidae

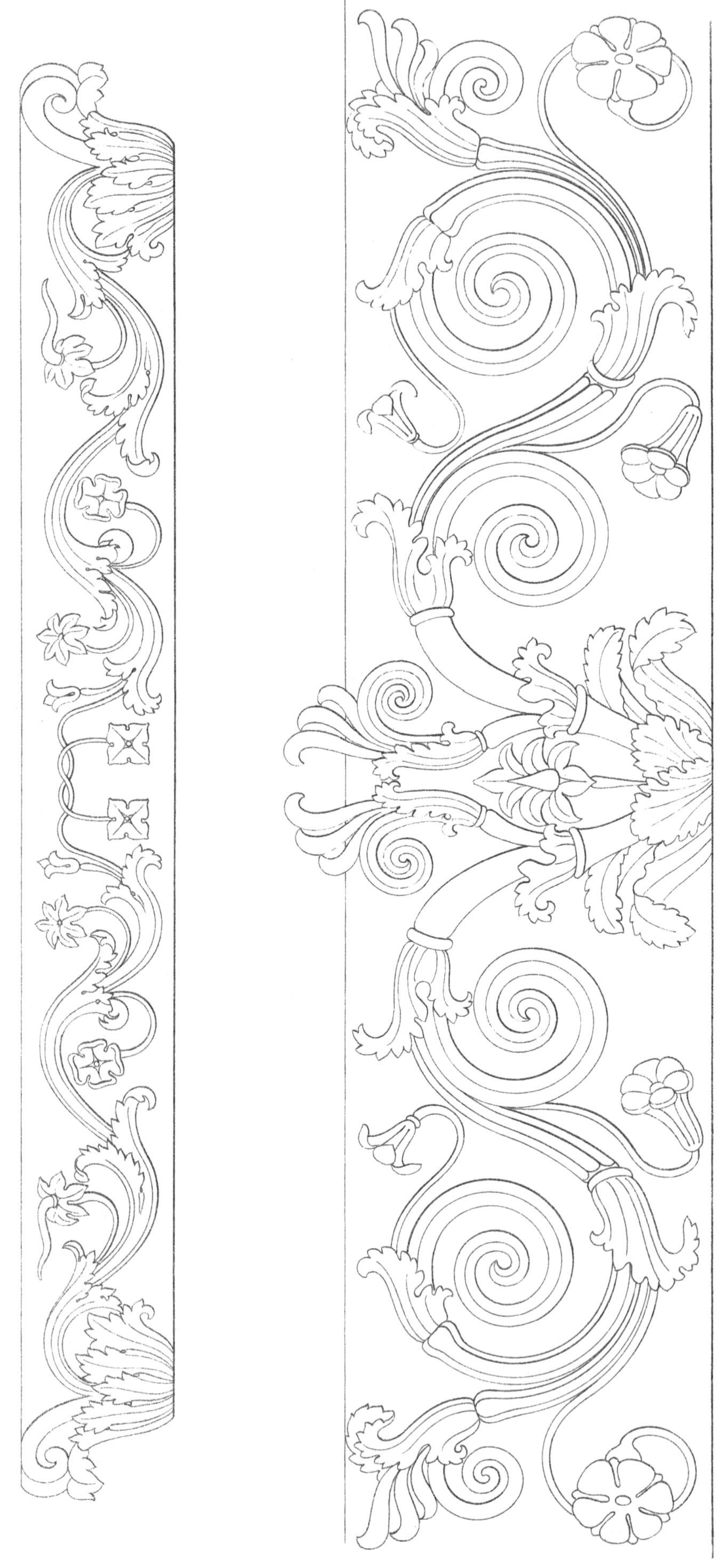

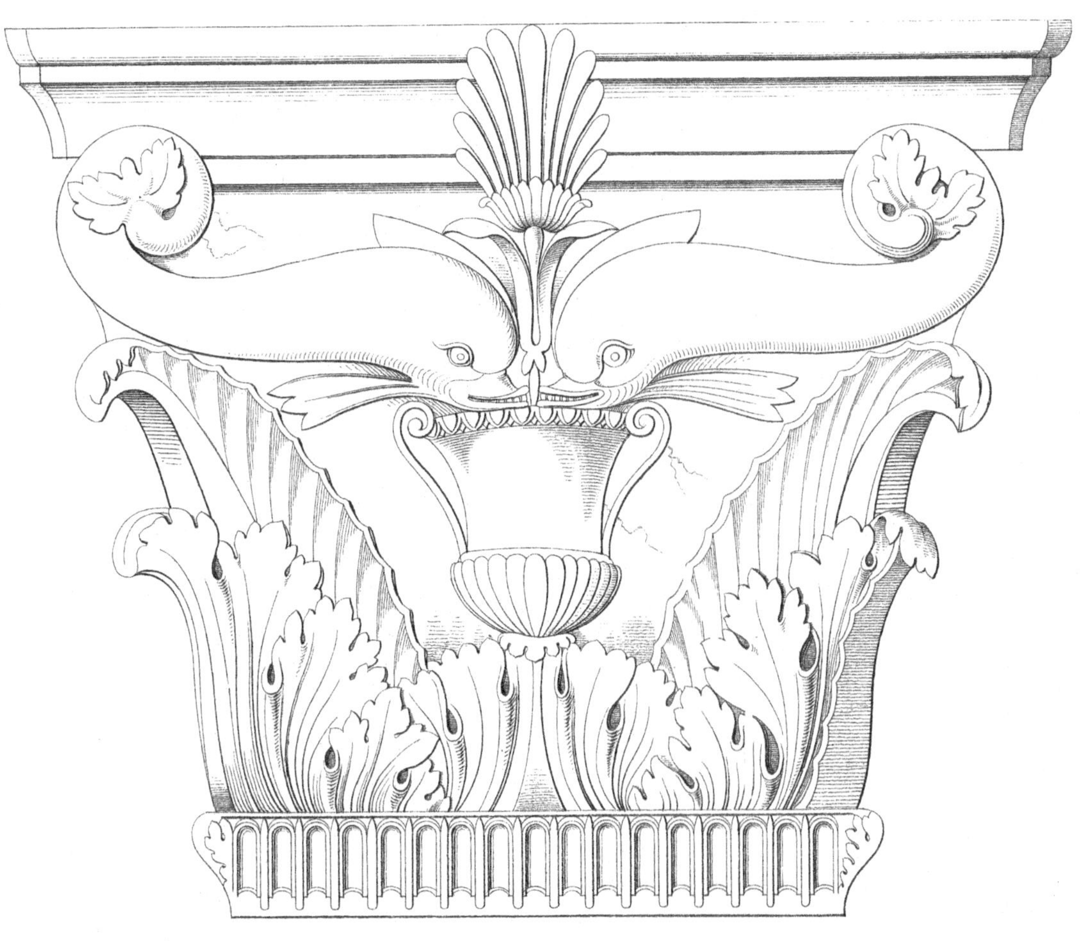

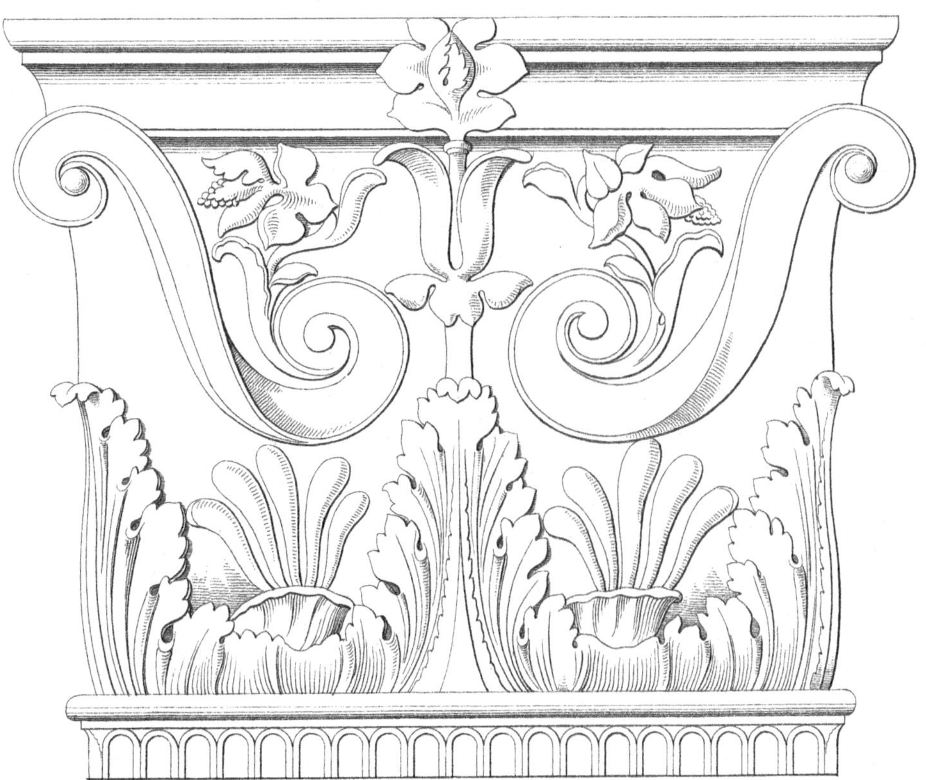

Antique pilaster of a capital, made at the same time as that of the Villa Poniatowski in Rome

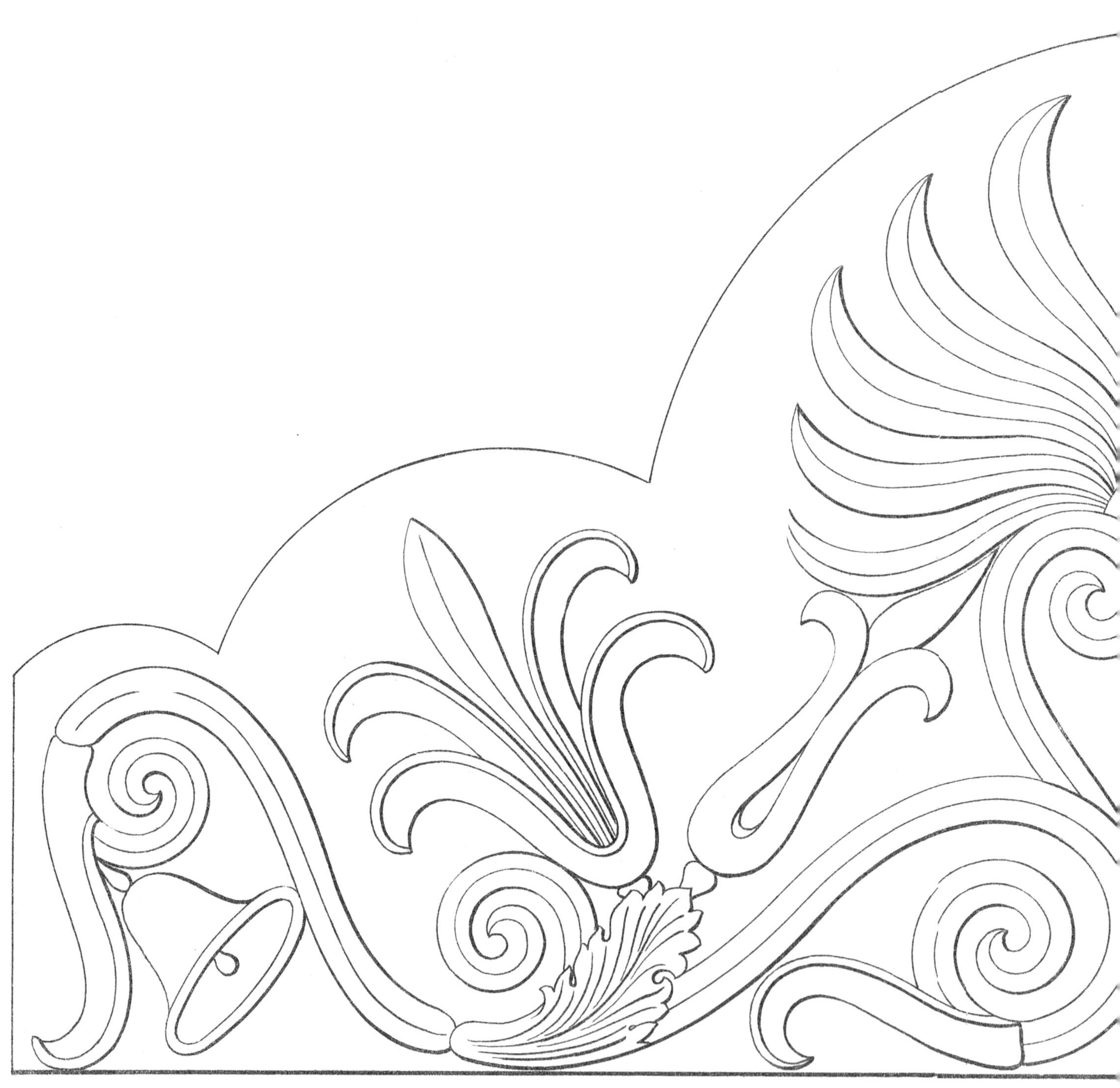

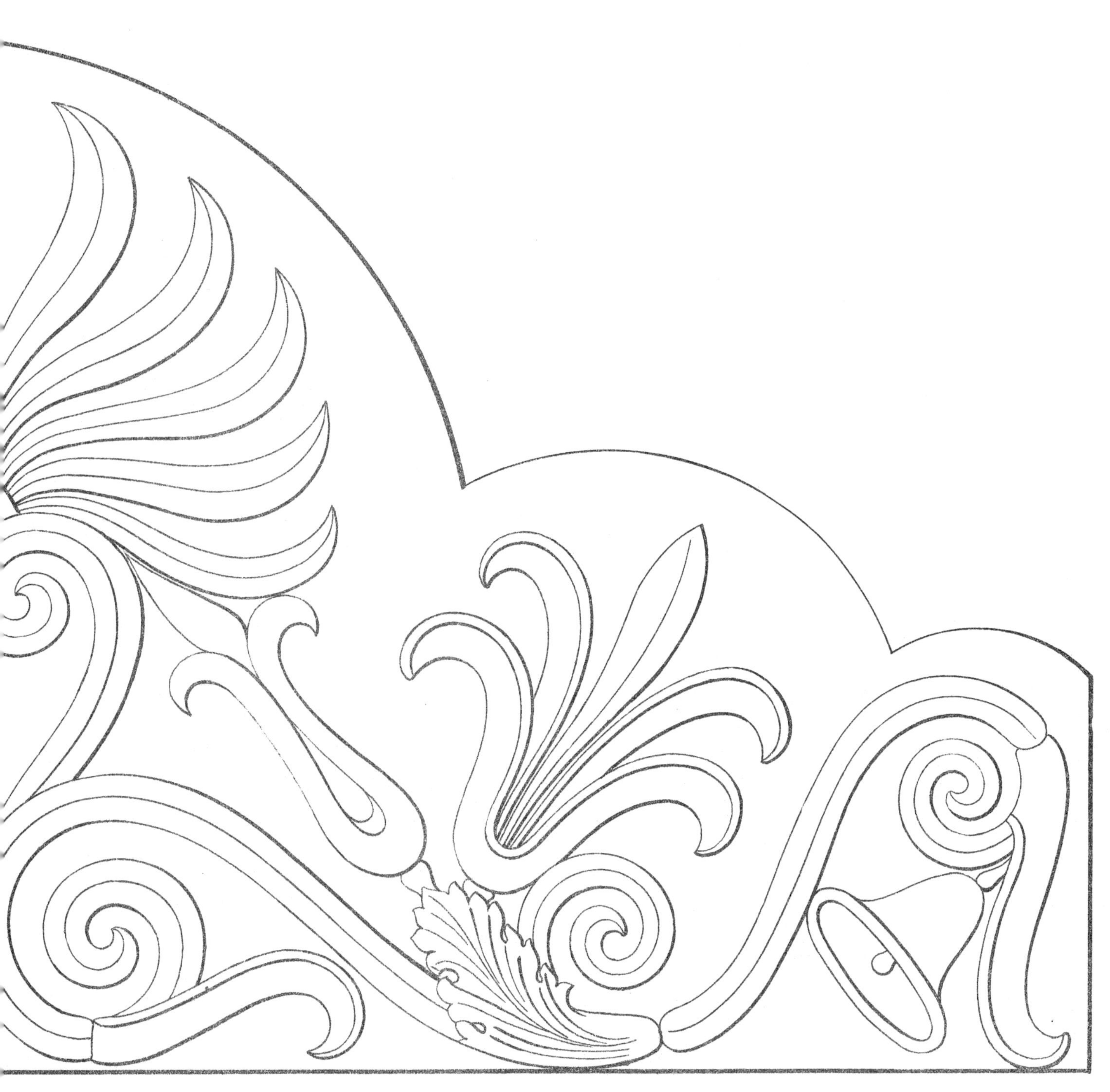

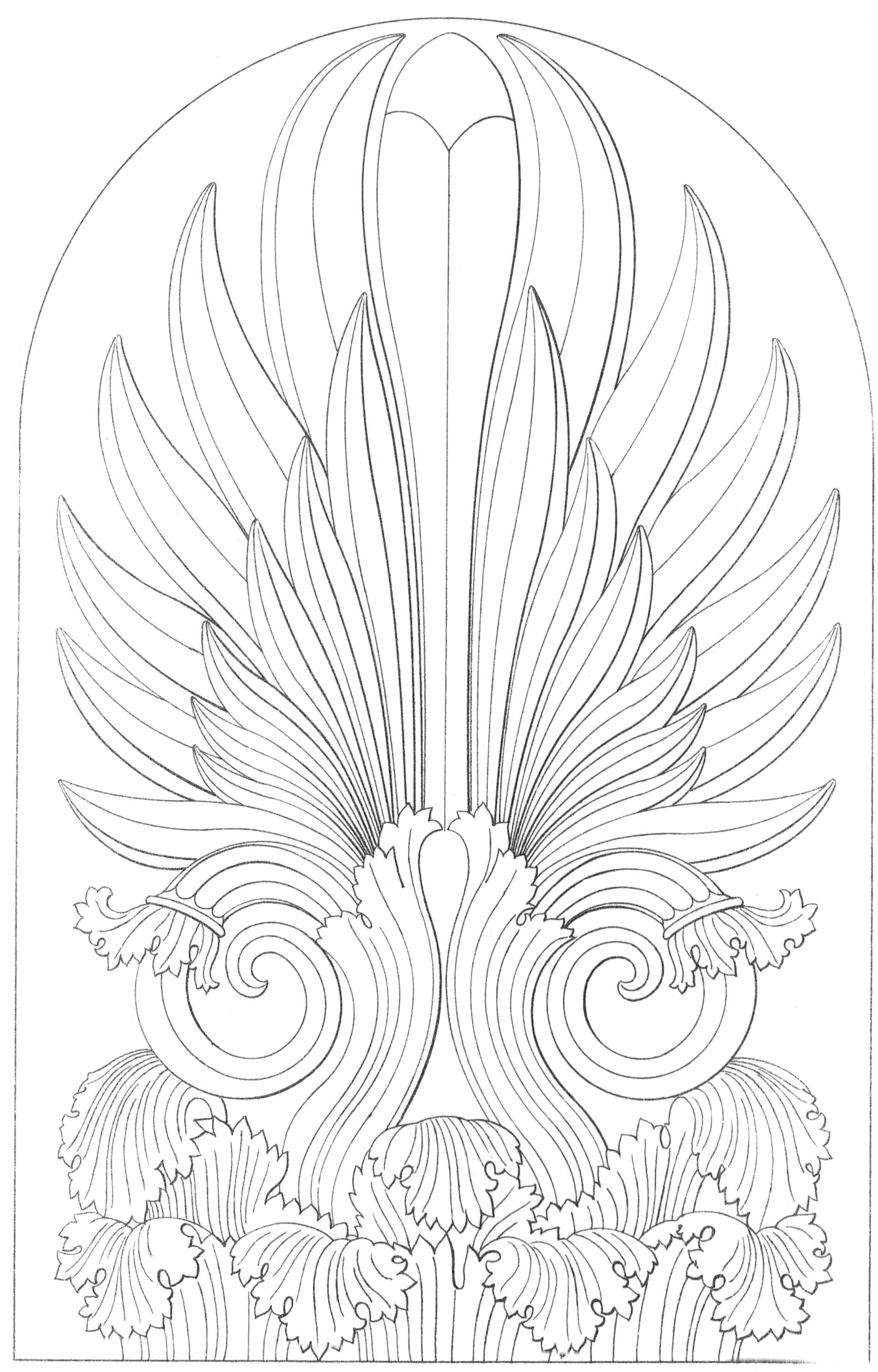

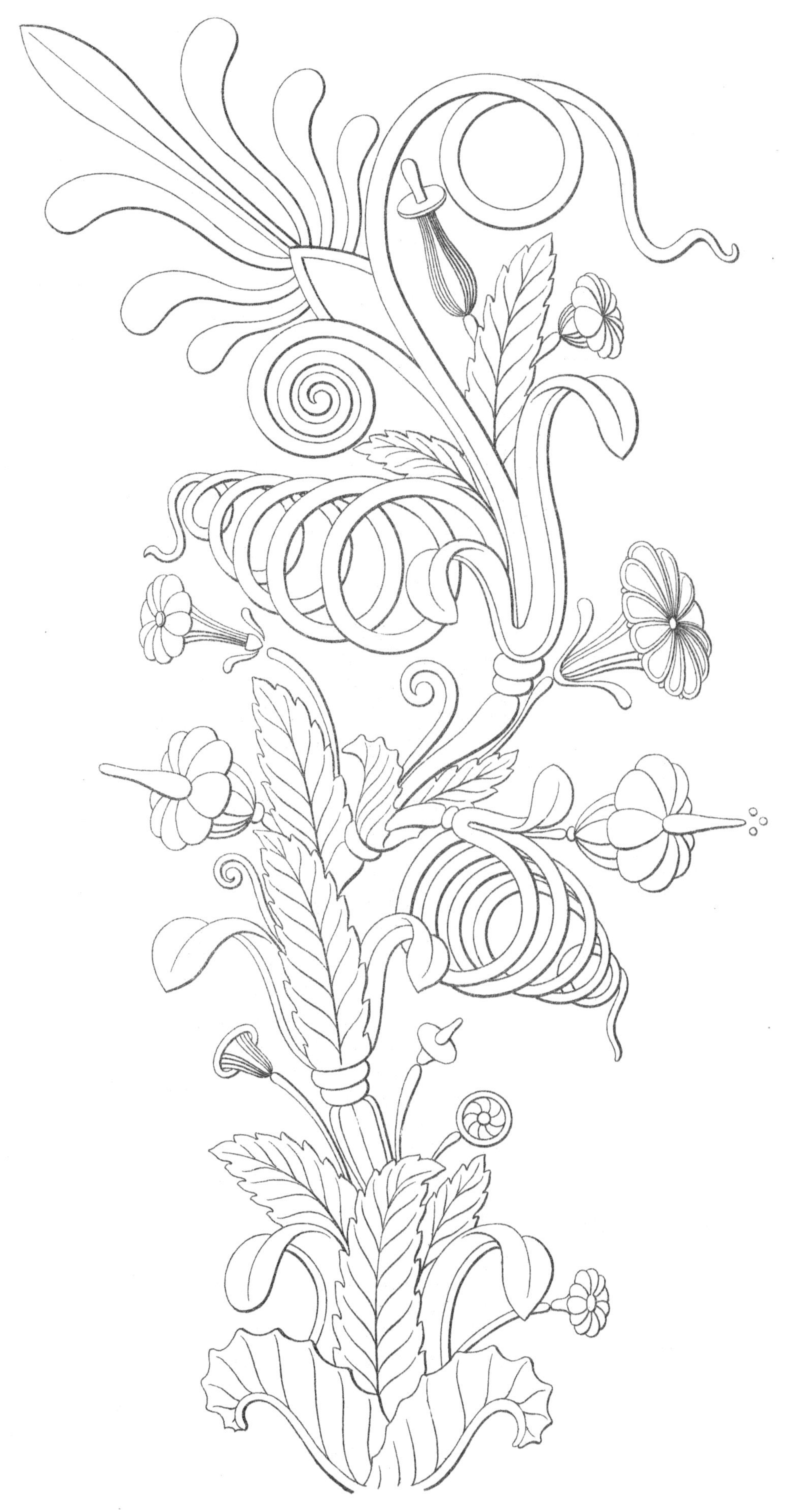

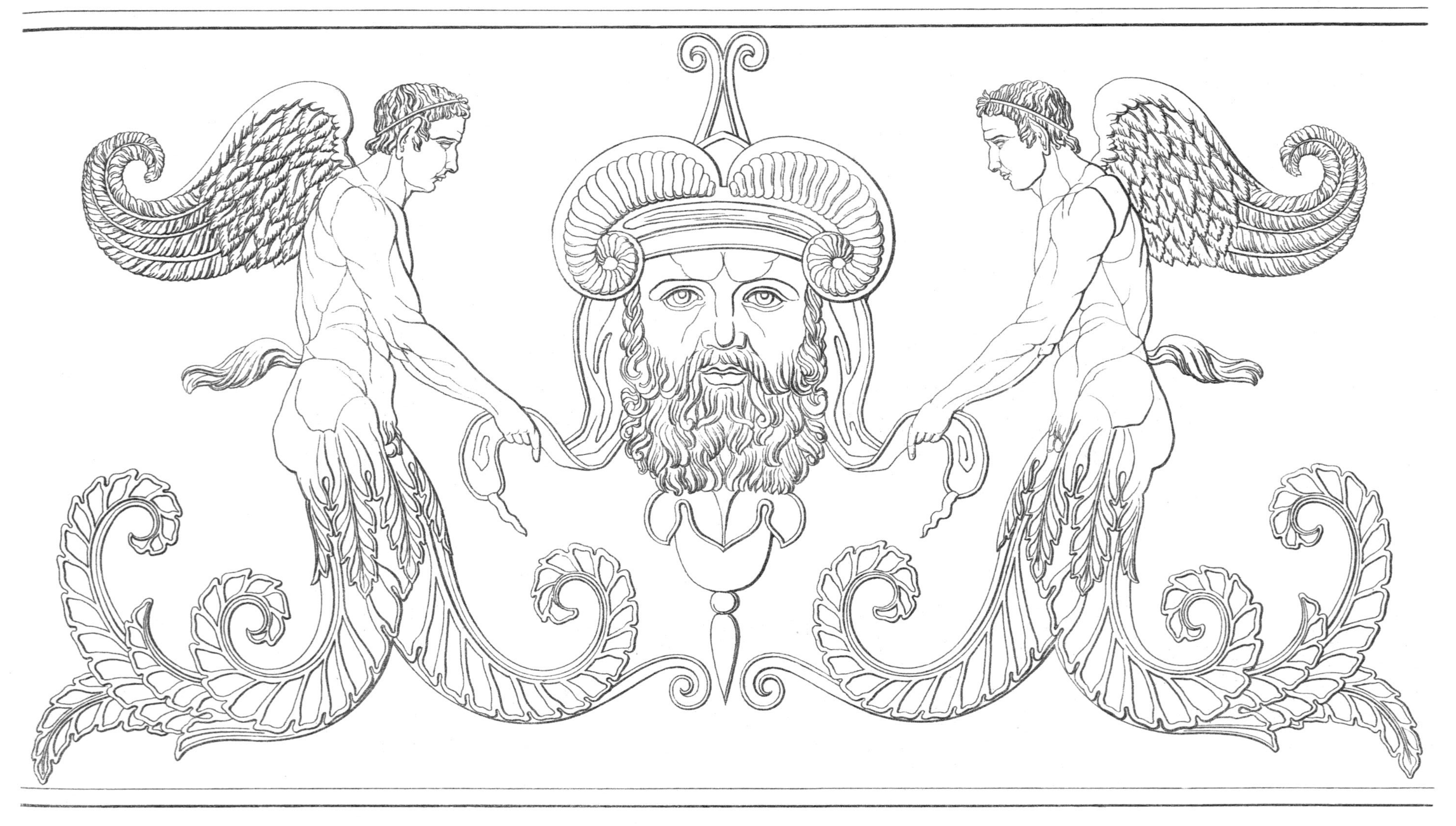

From the Kircherian Museum

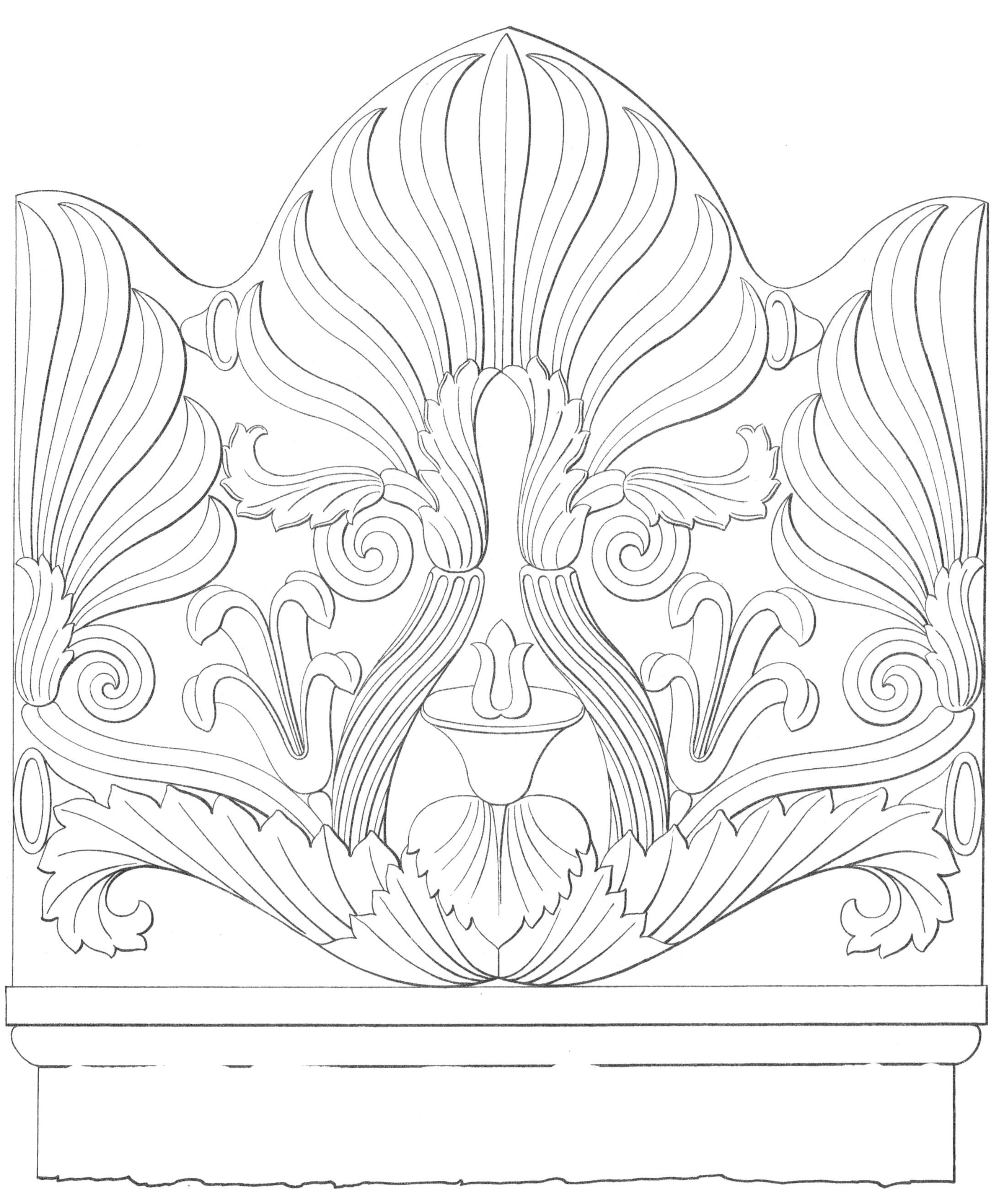

In Athens

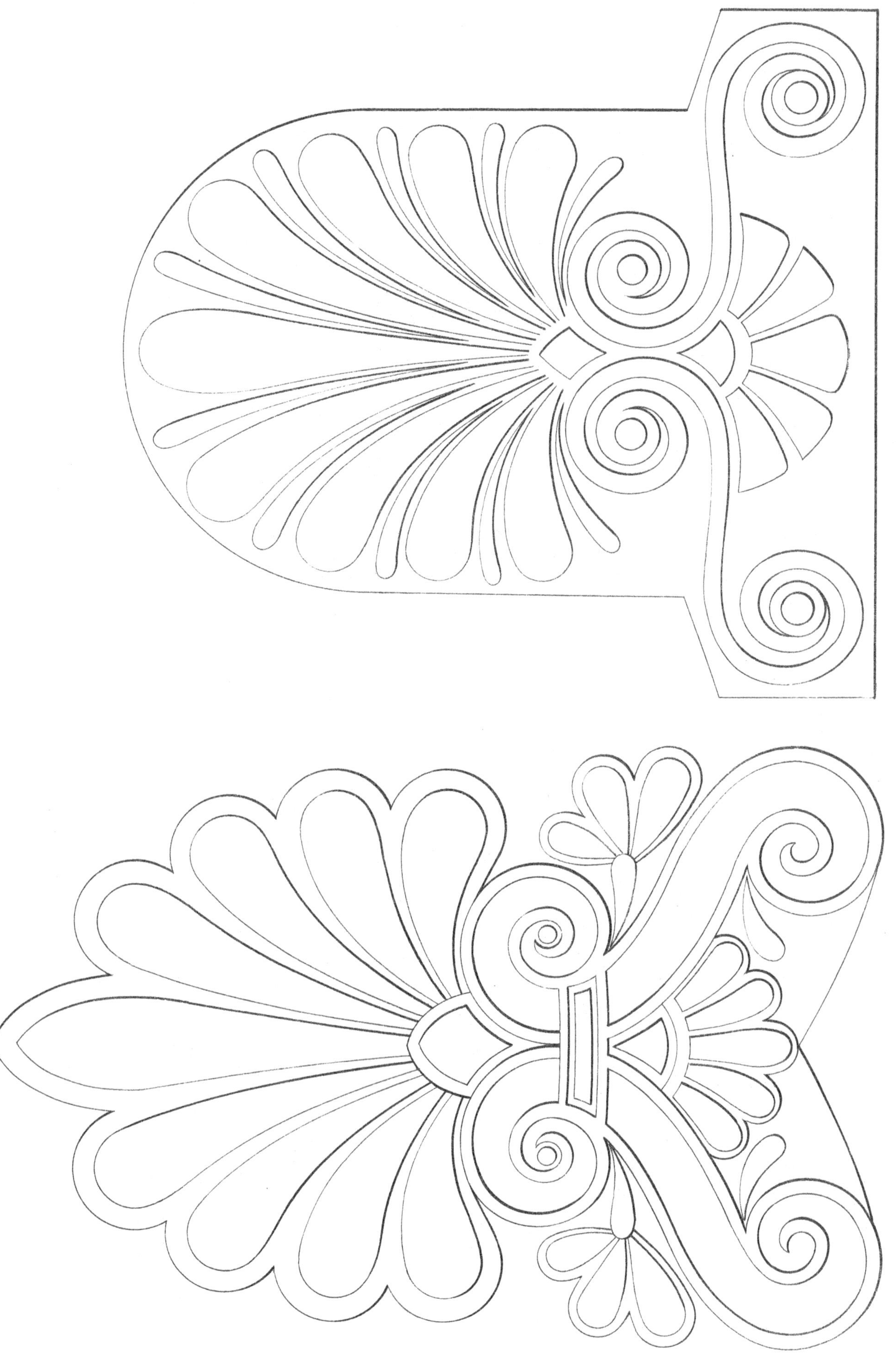

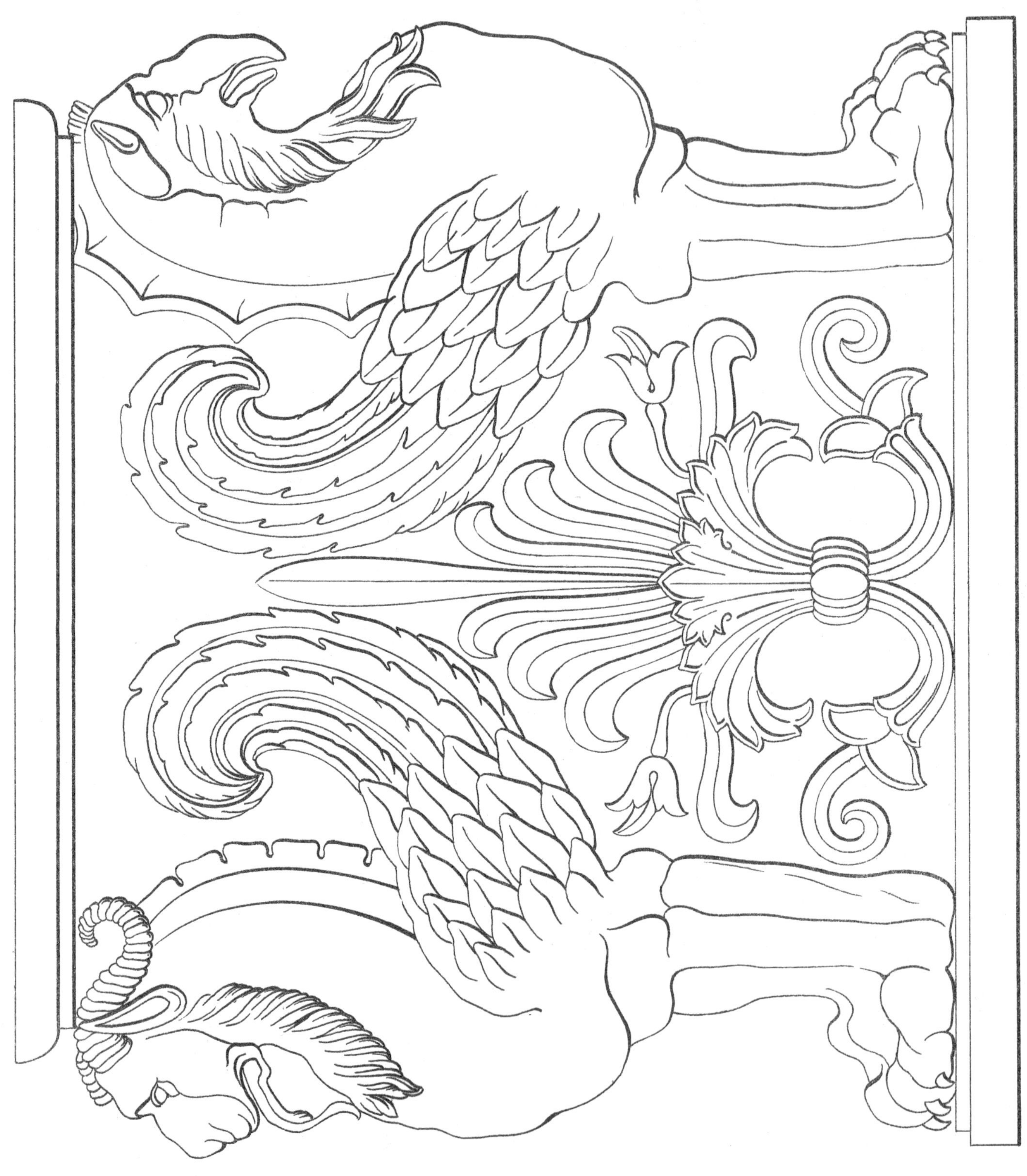

Plate 43

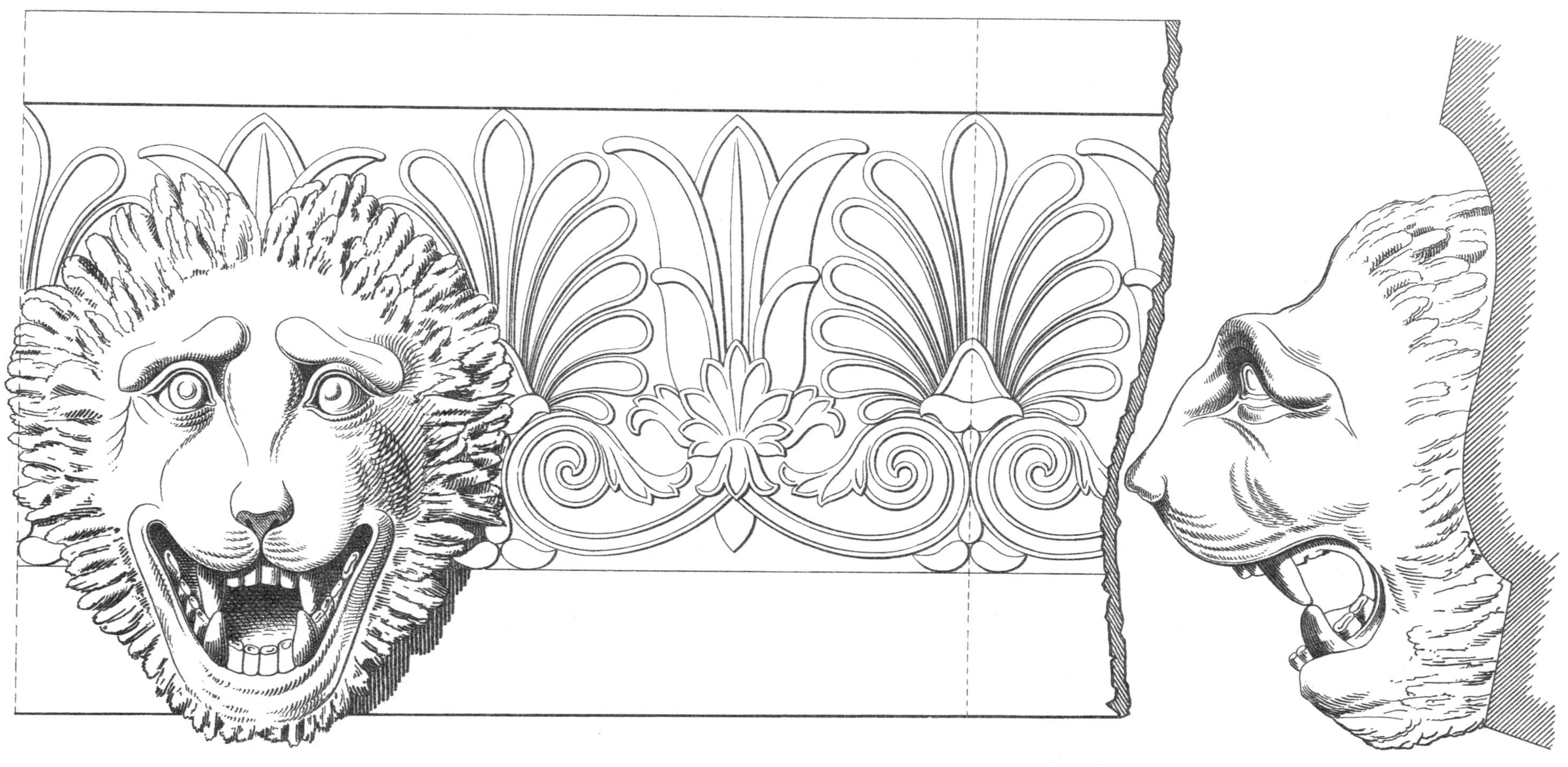

Modeled on a marble fragment in Athens

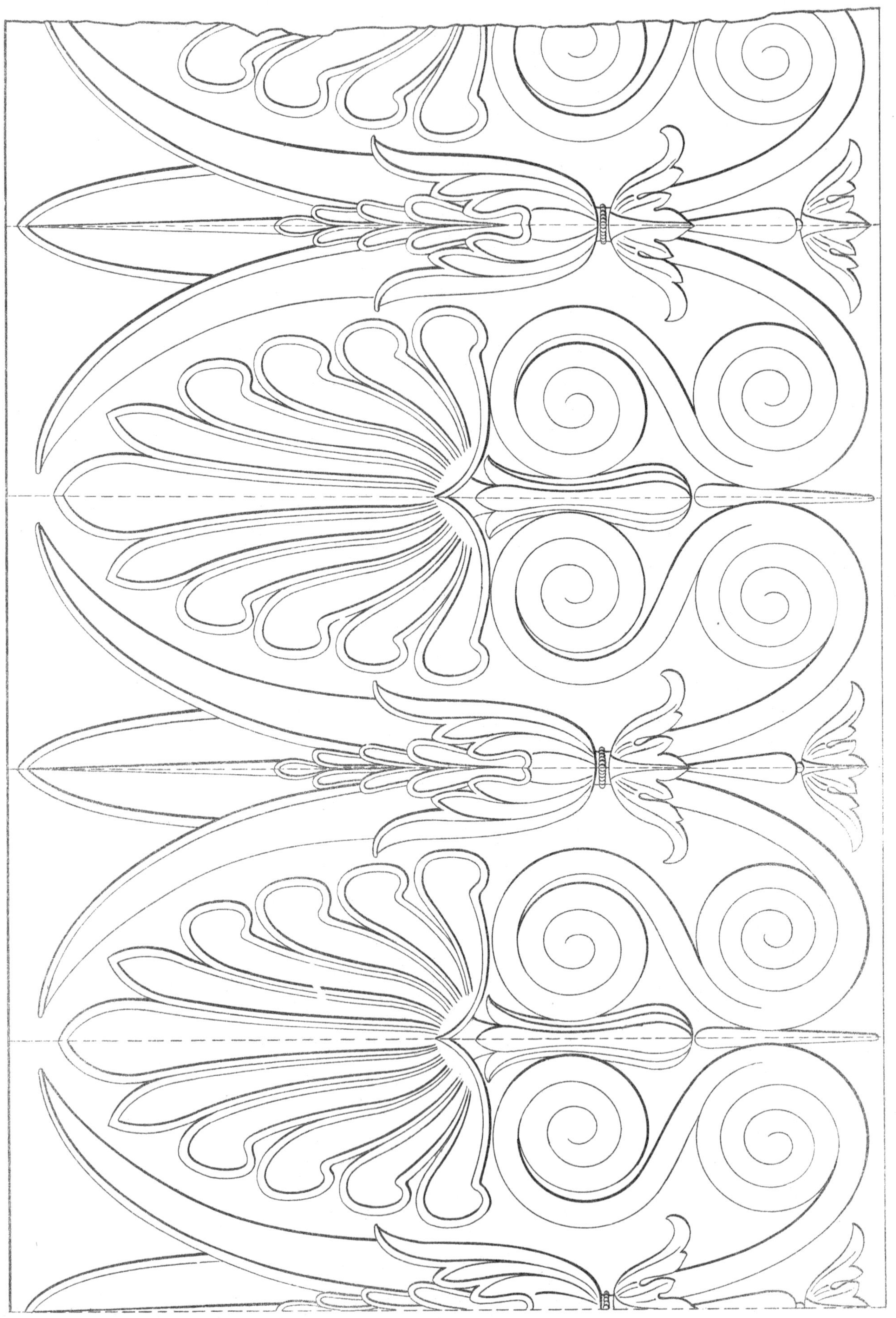

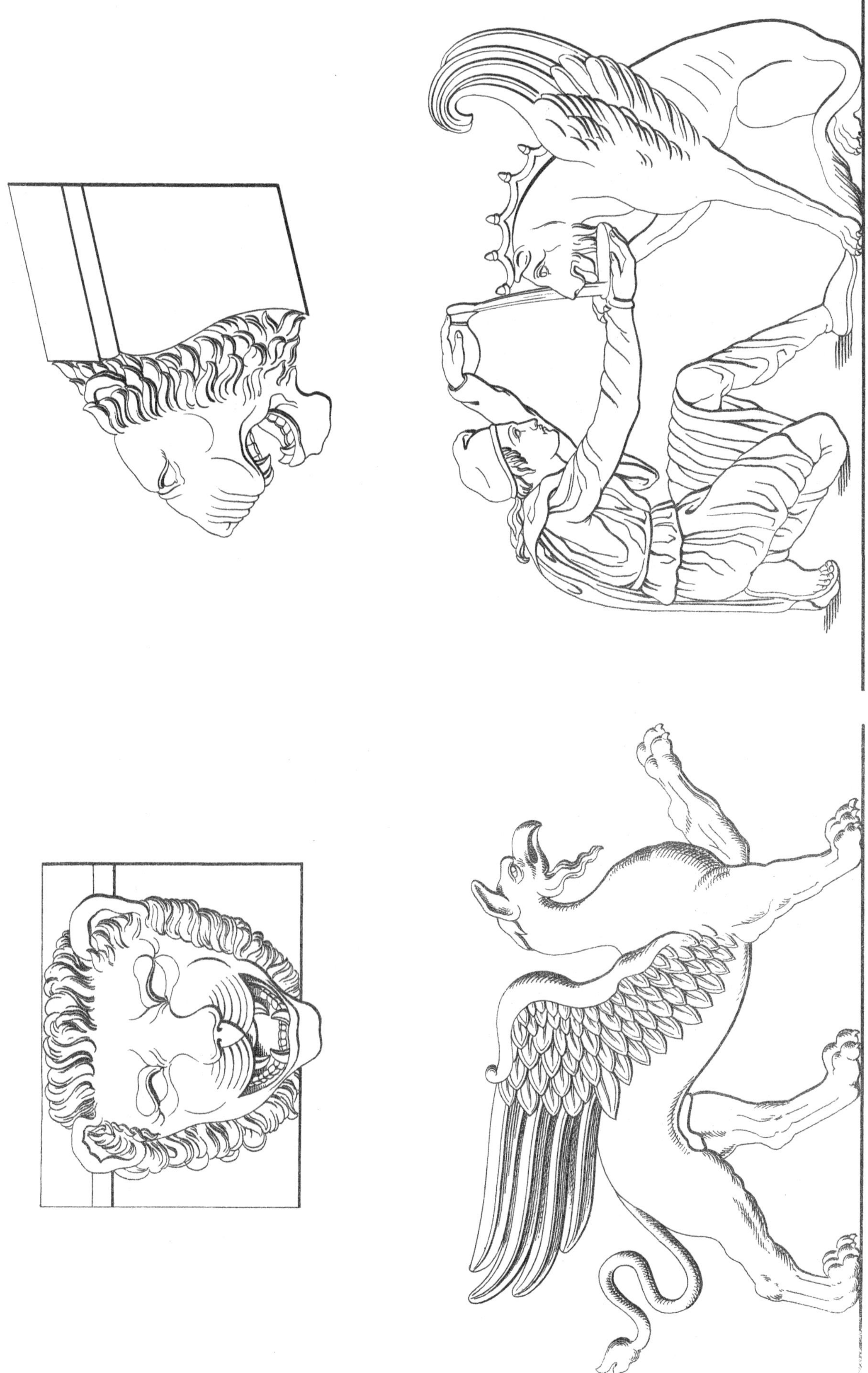

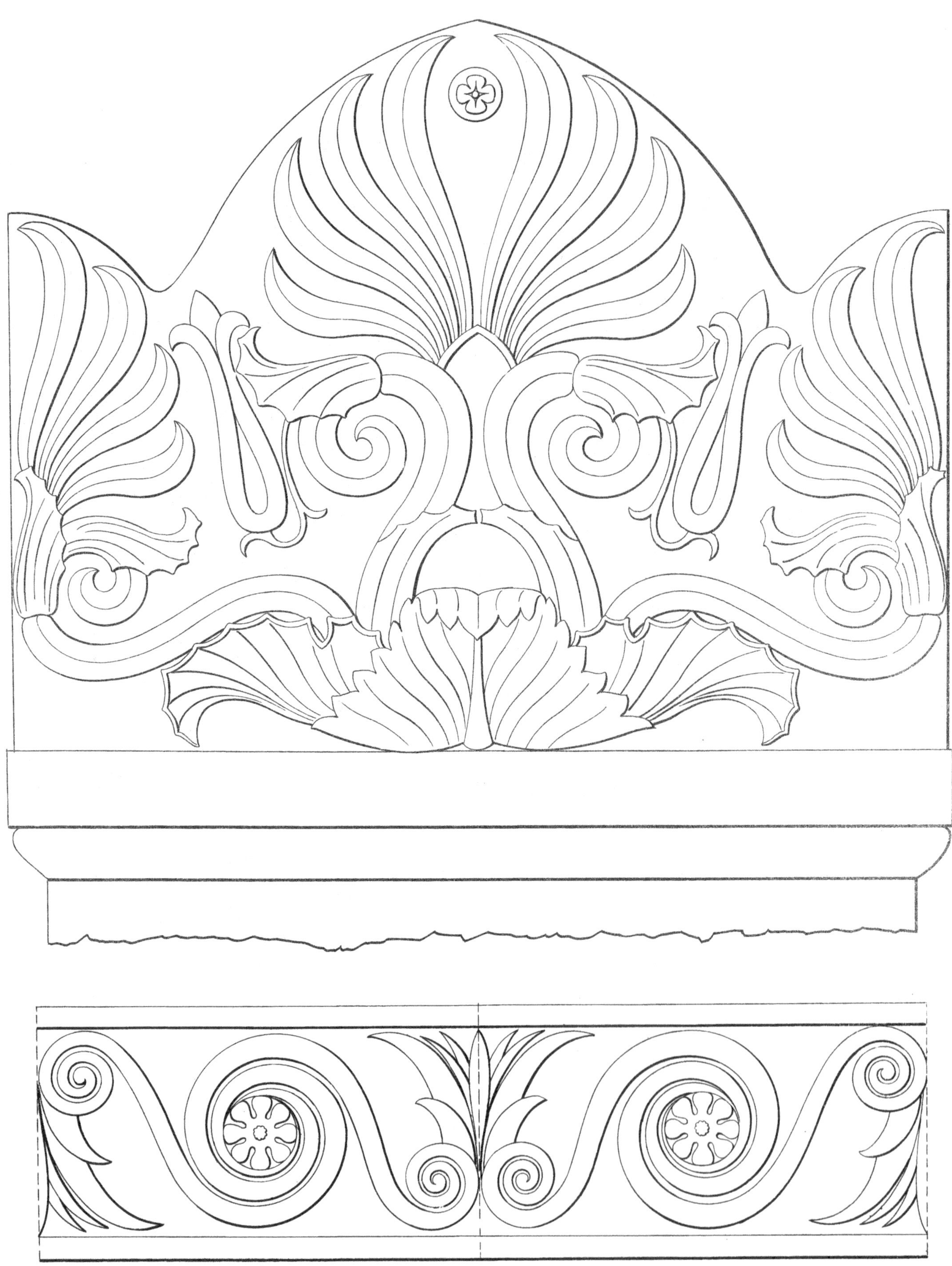

Plate 47

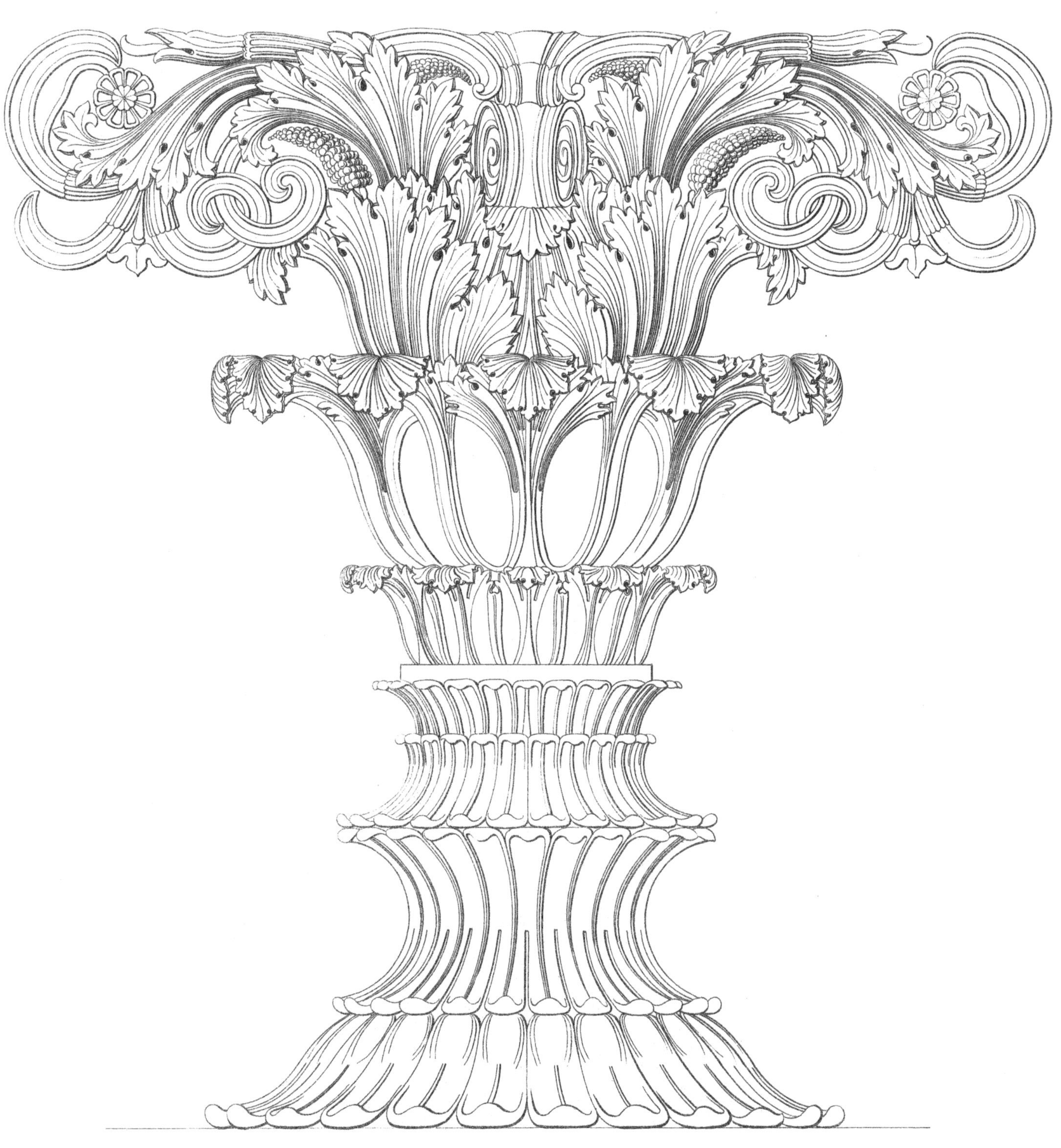

Cap of the monument to Lysicrates in Athens

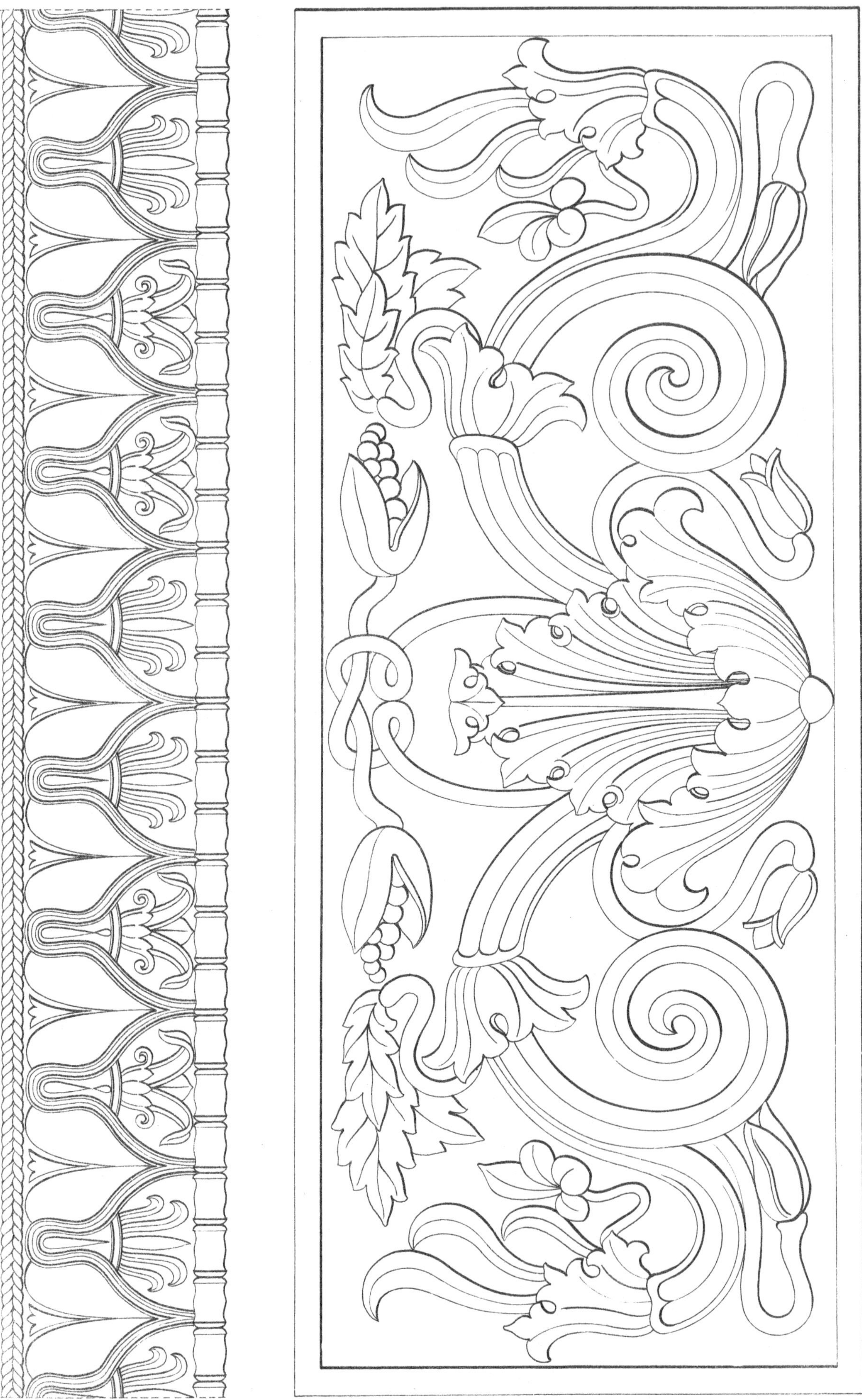

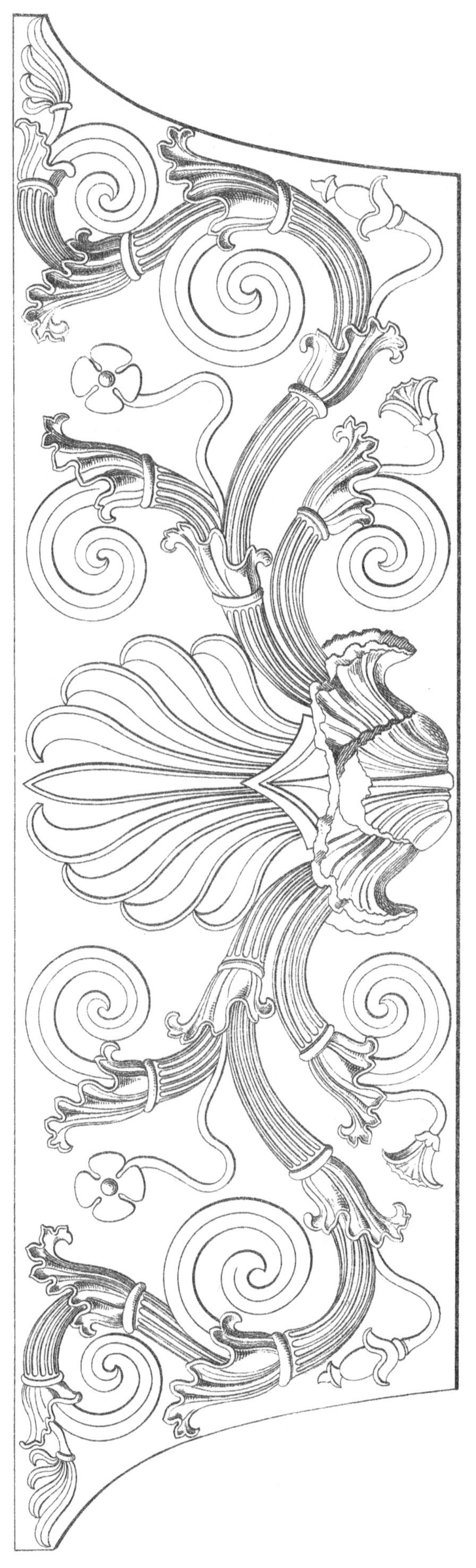

Front of a capital on the temple of Apollo
(Didimaeus of Branchidae)

In Branchidae

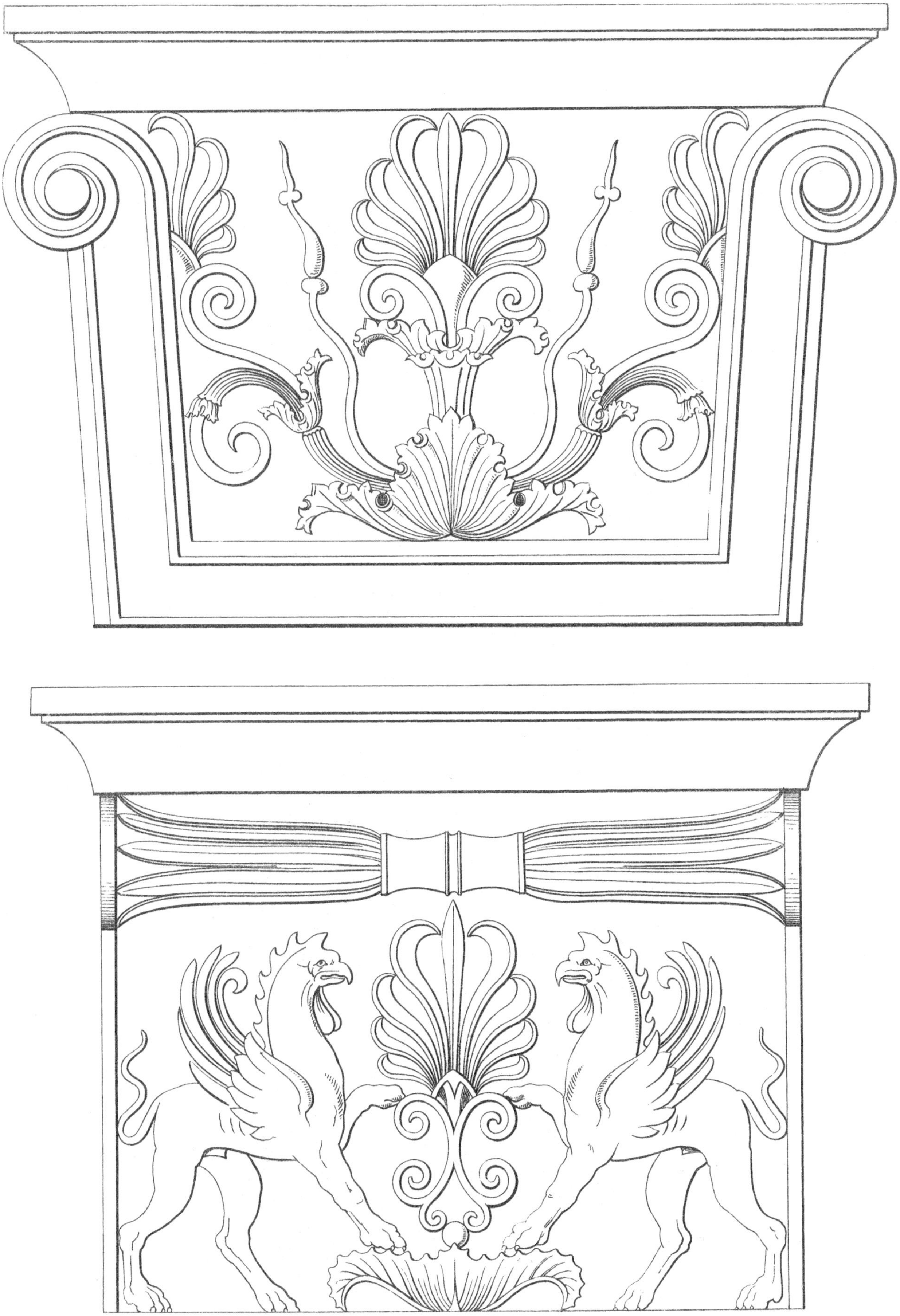

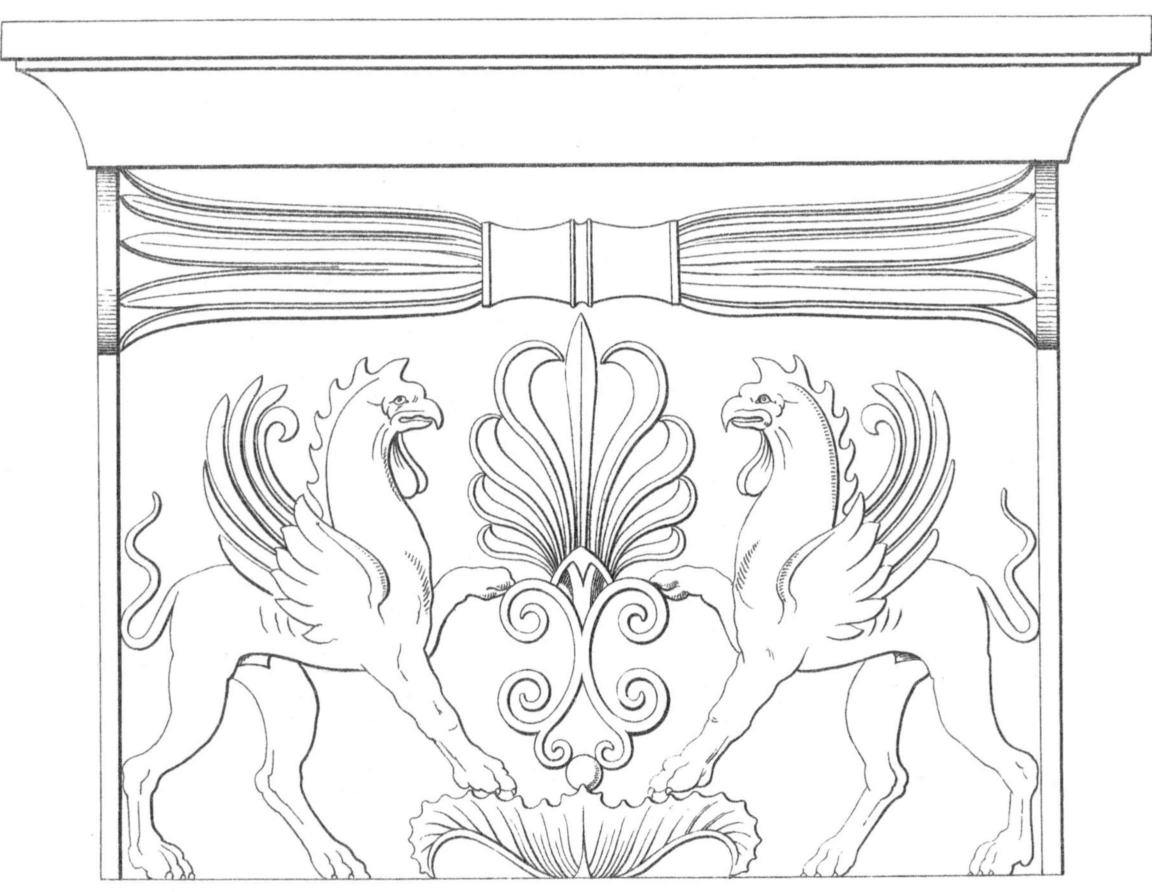

Pilaster capitals from the ruins of Pirelle

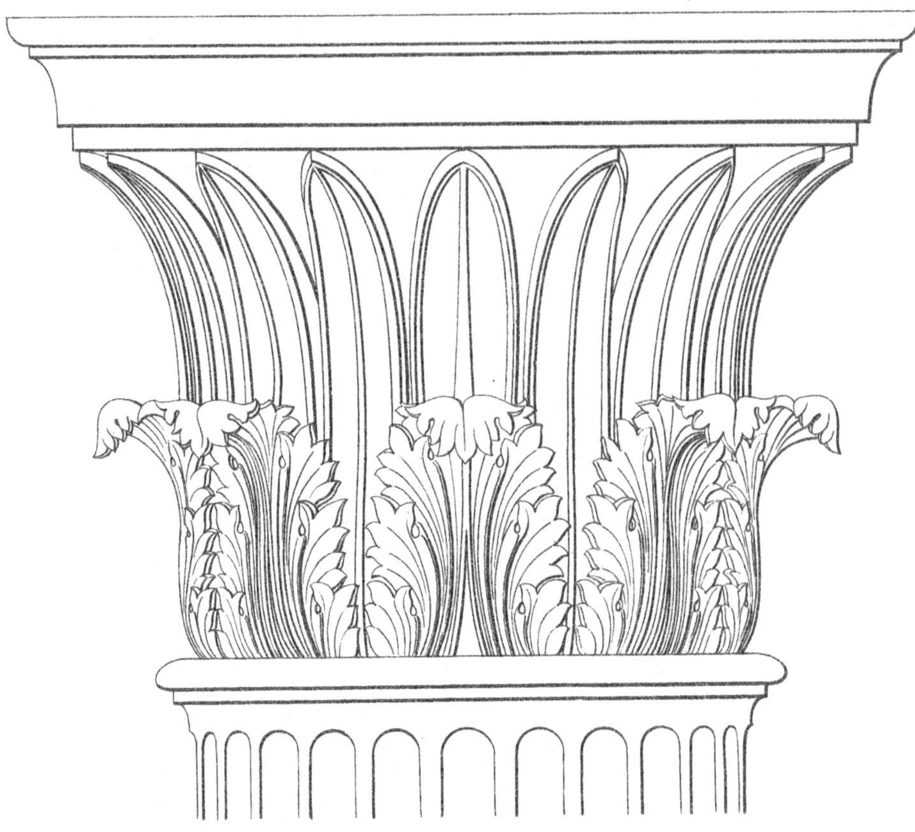

From the wind tower in Athens

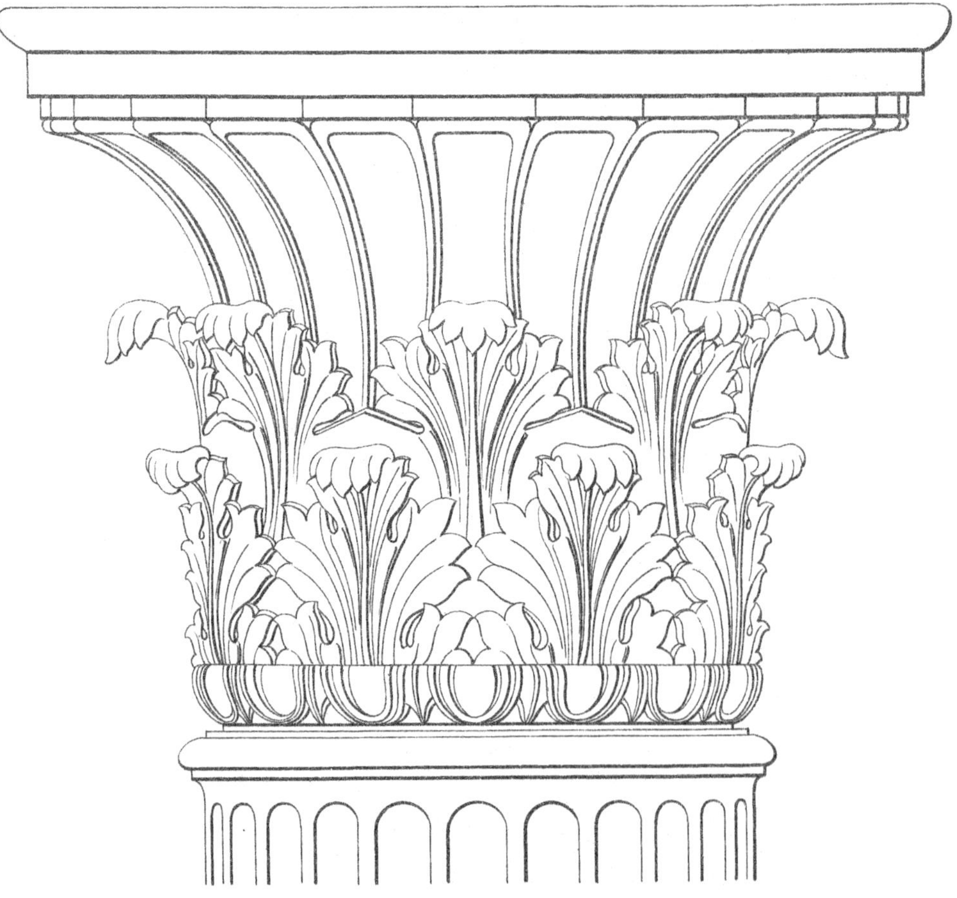

Found on the island of Milo

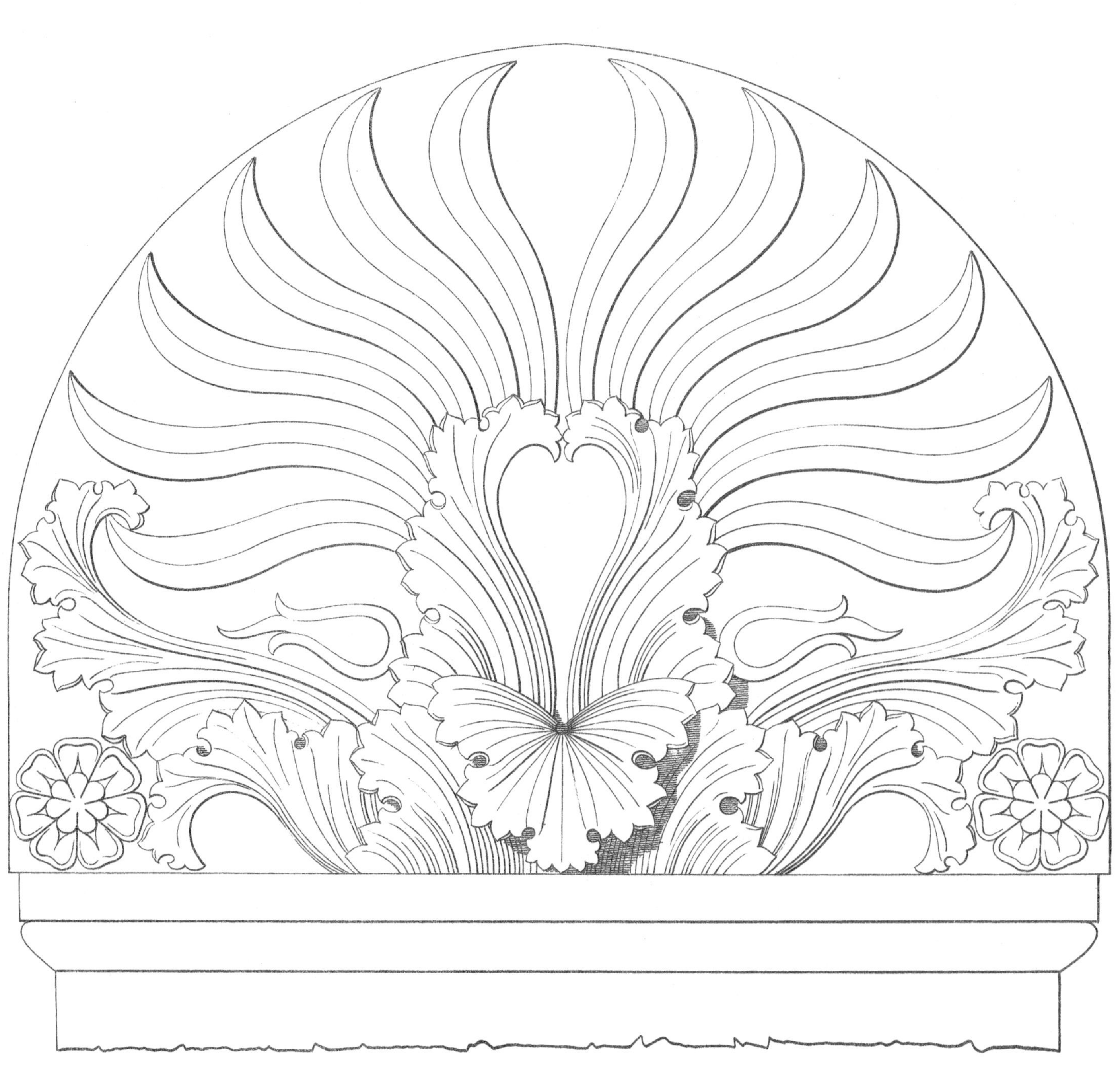

In Athens, in the house of Giacomo

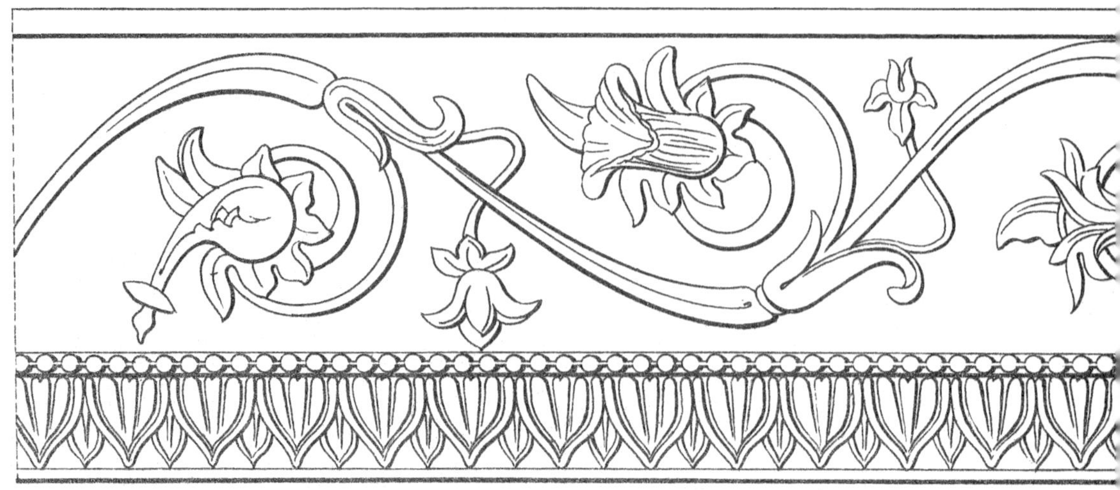

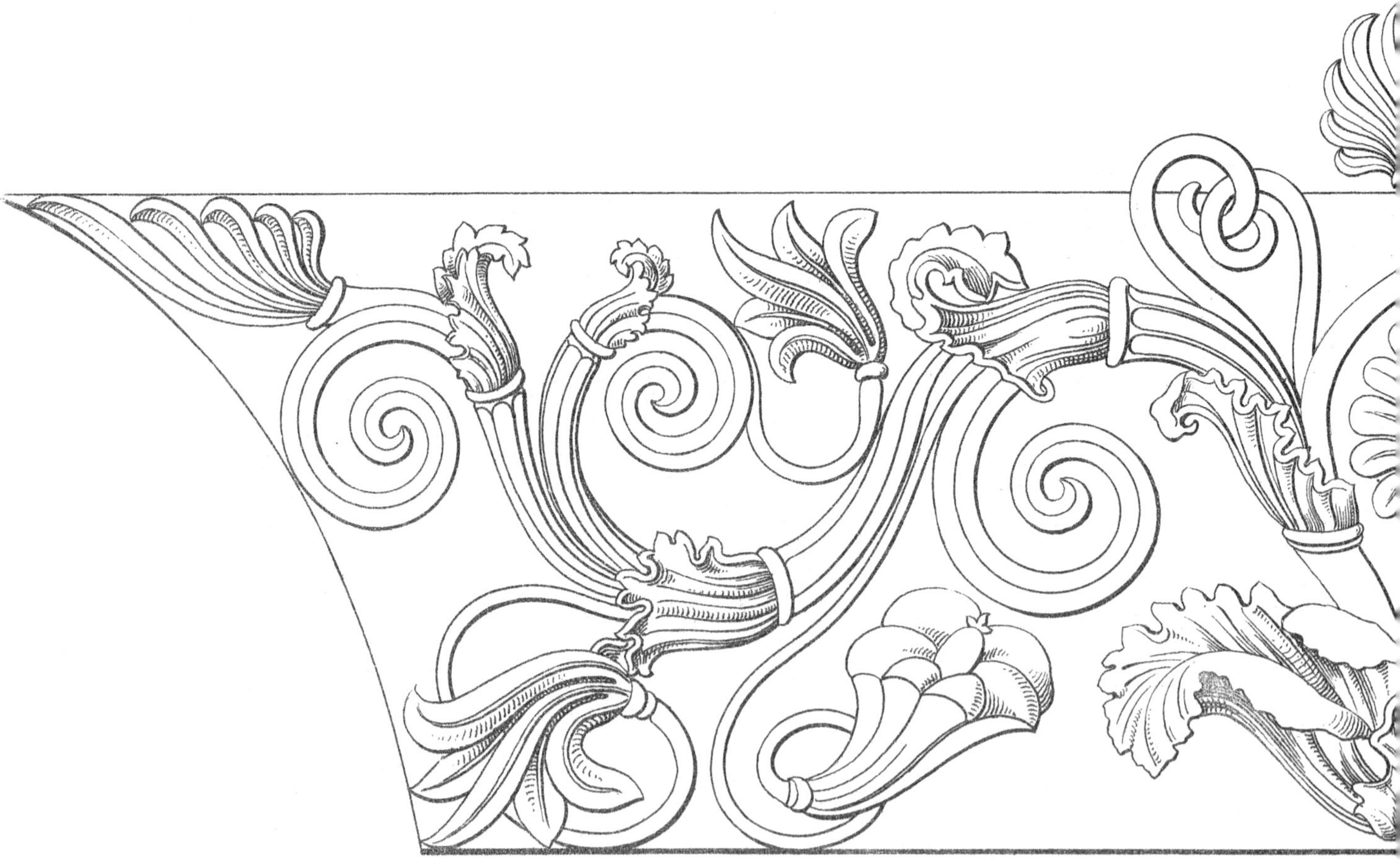

PLATE 55

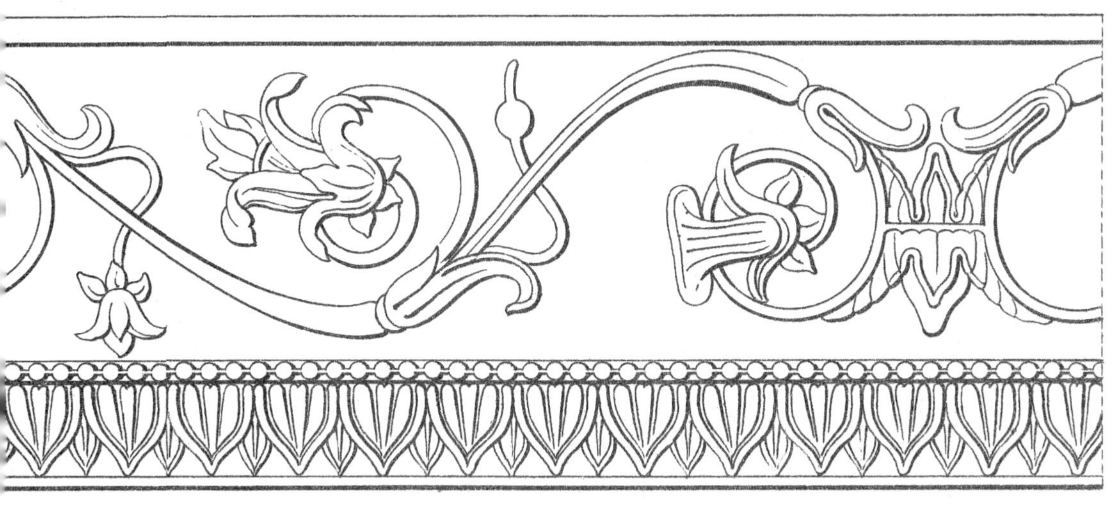

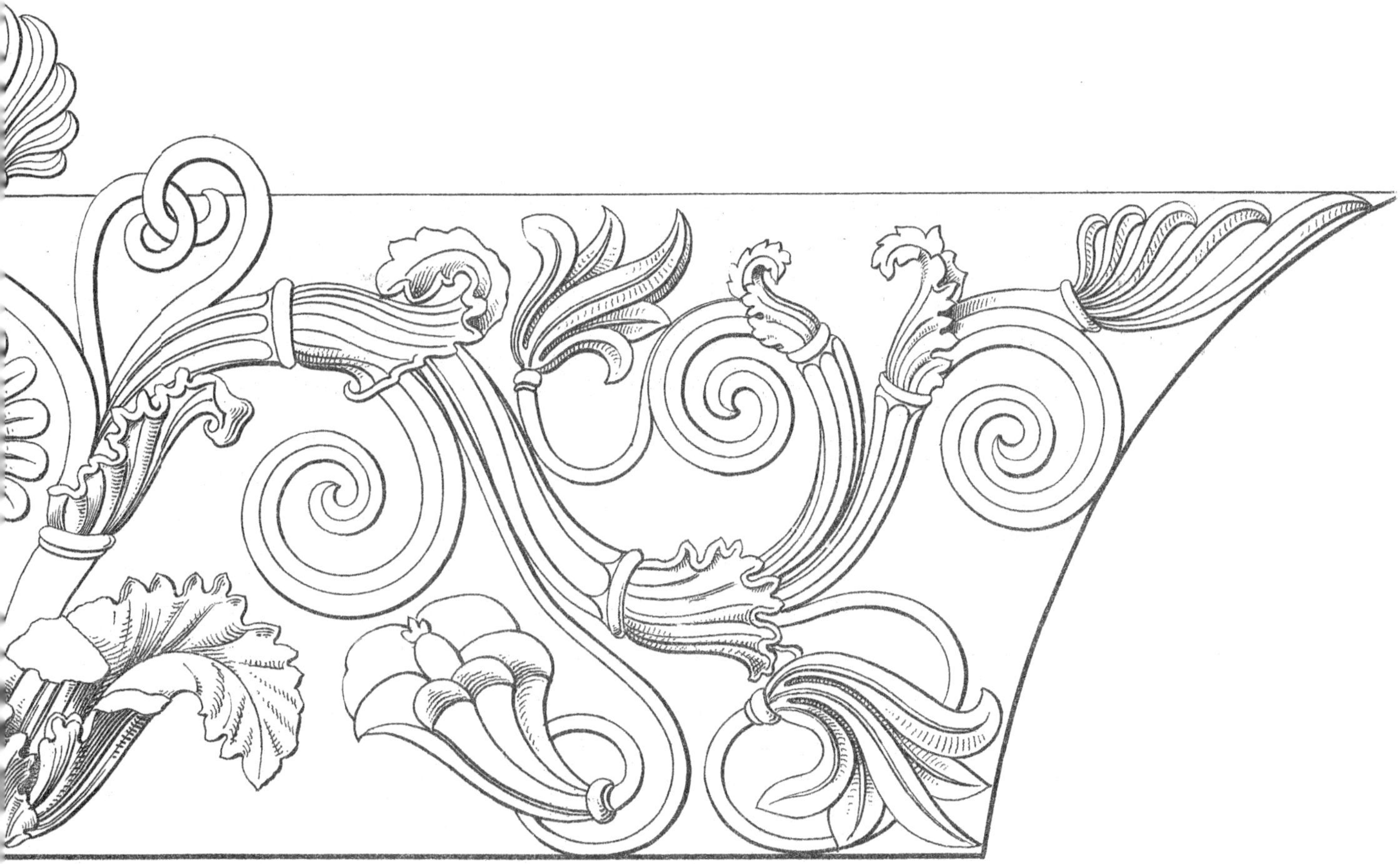

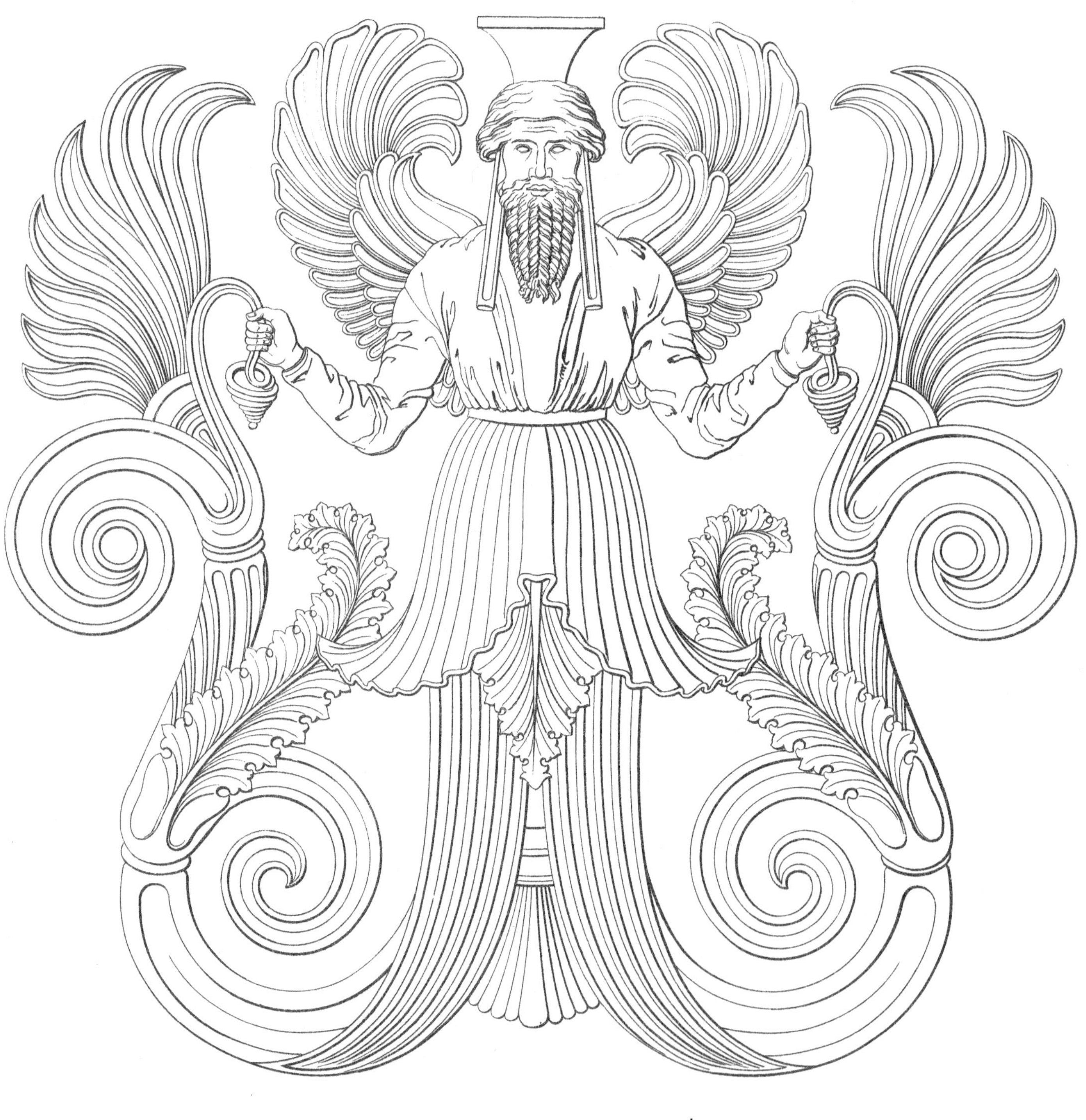

Plate 56

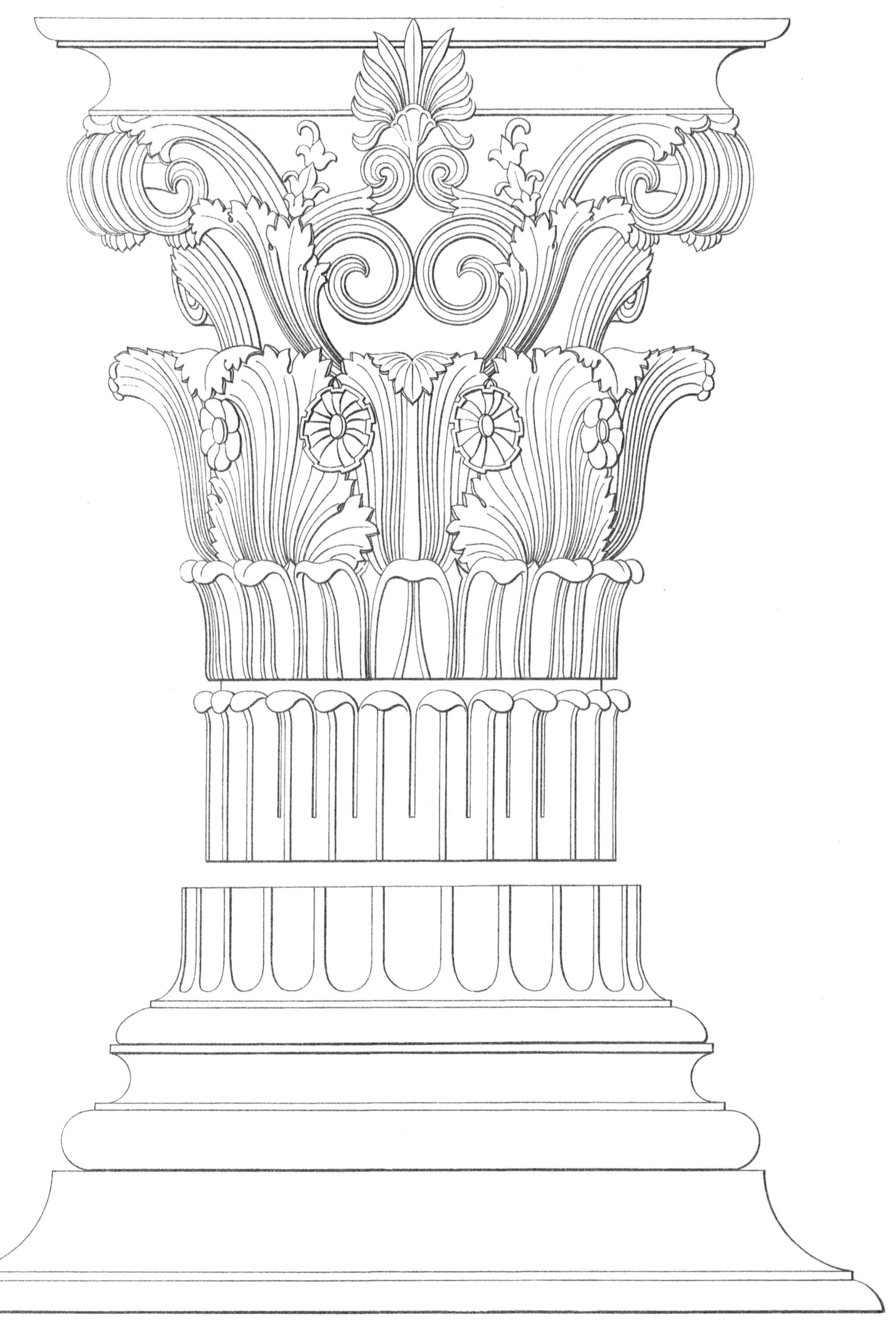

Plate 57

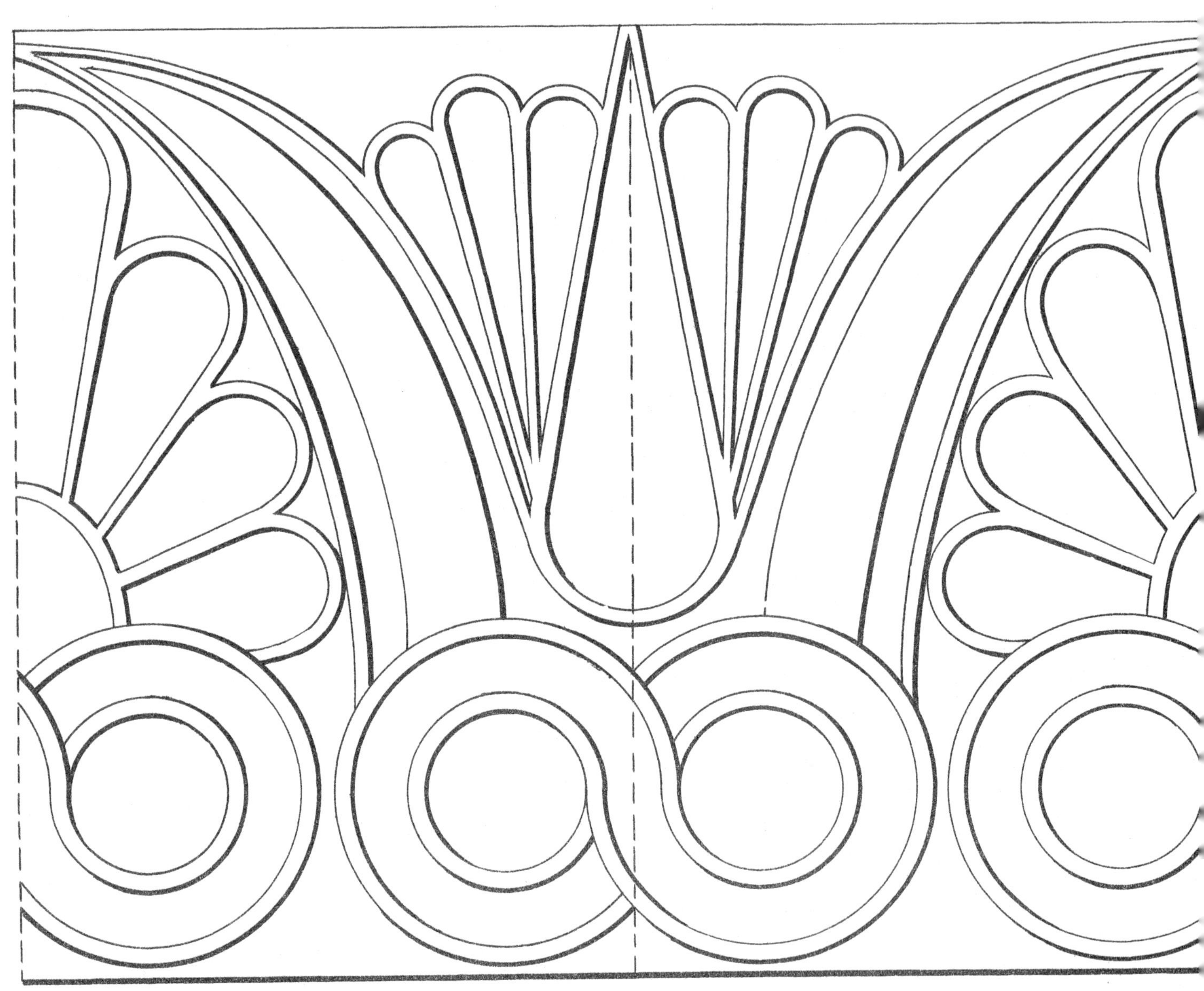

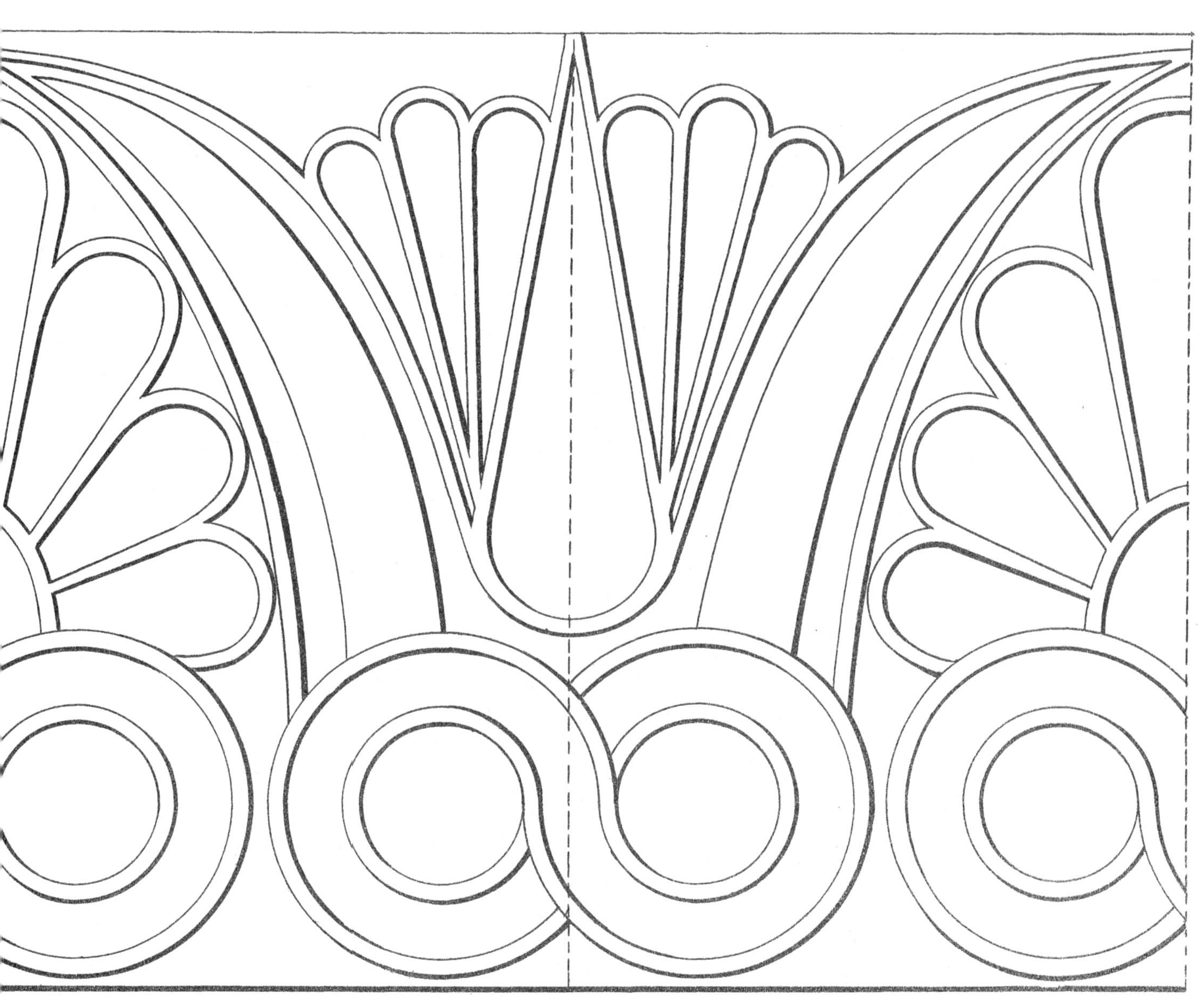

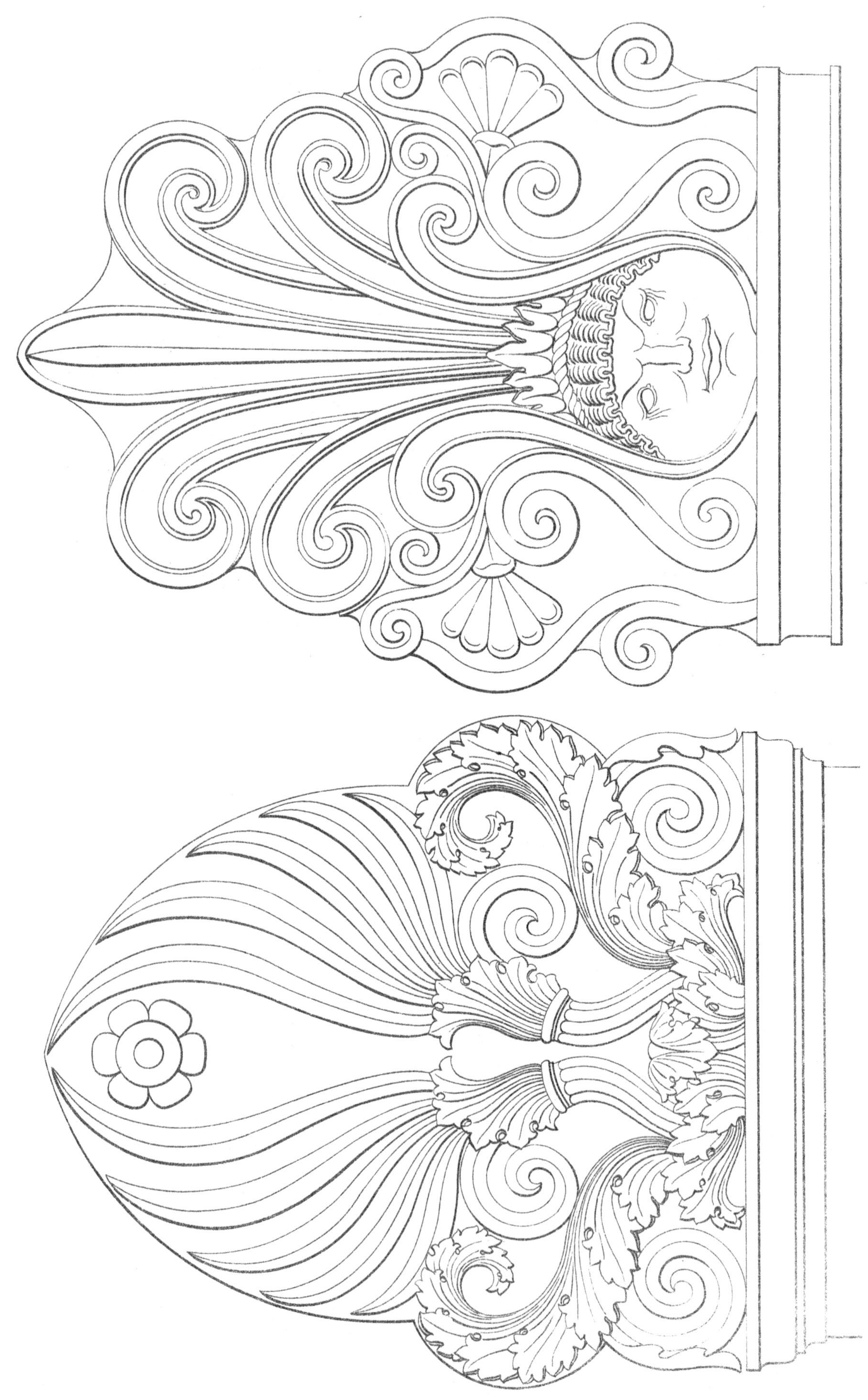

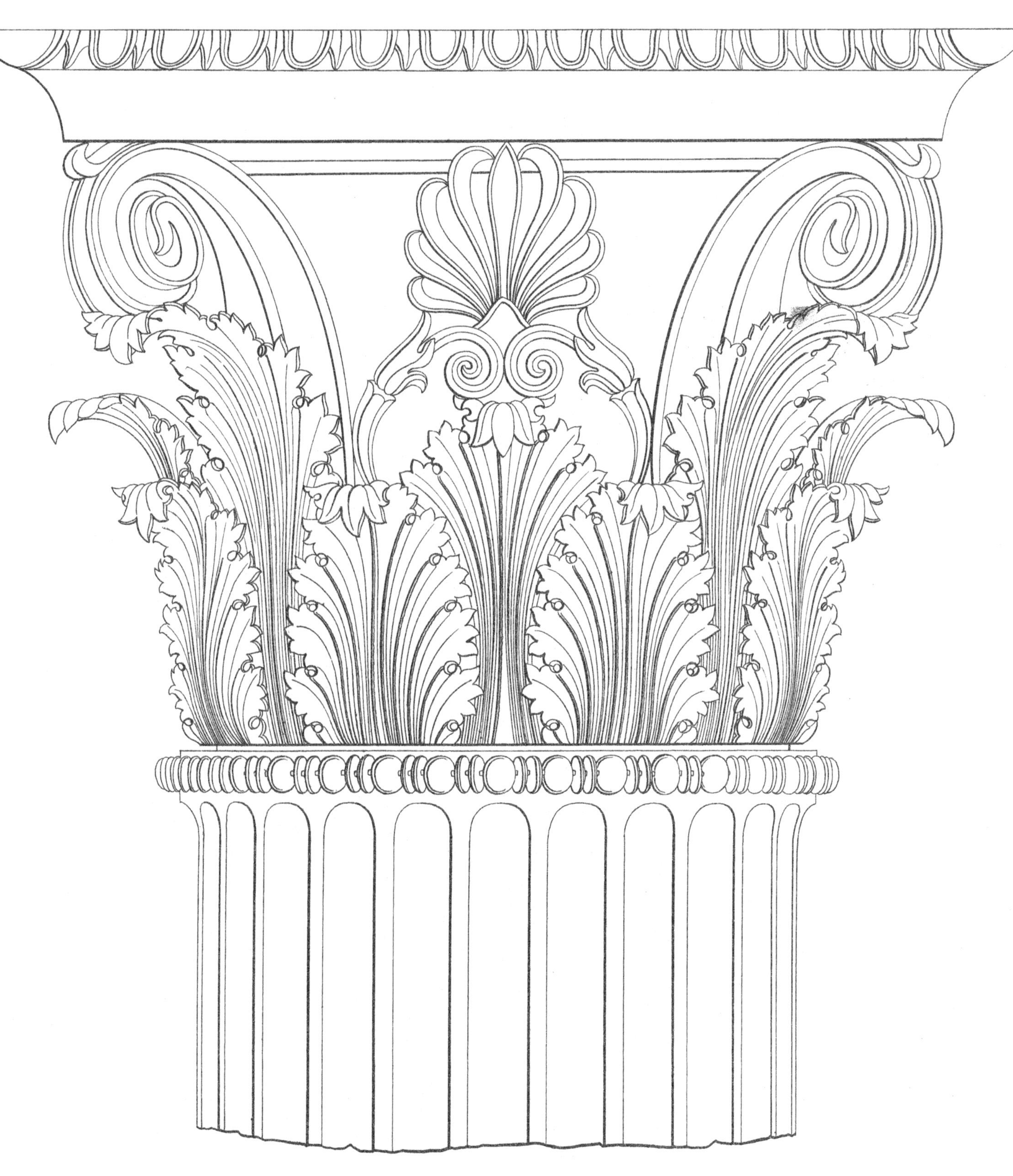

Capital in the temple of Apollo in Miletus

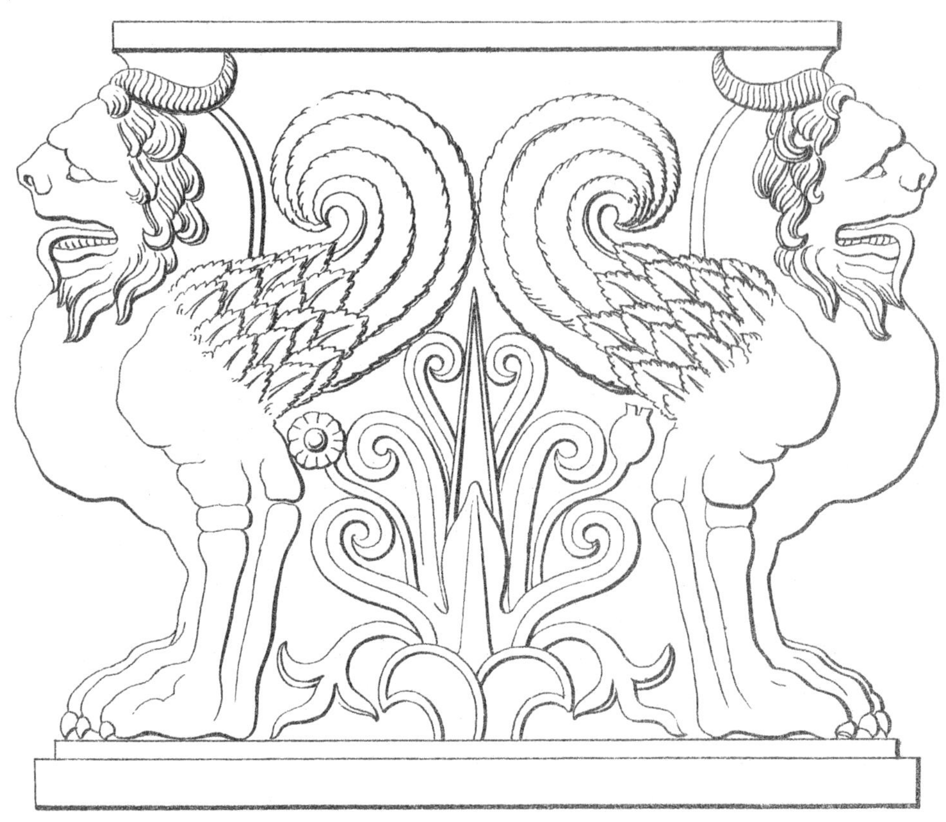

Antique chair

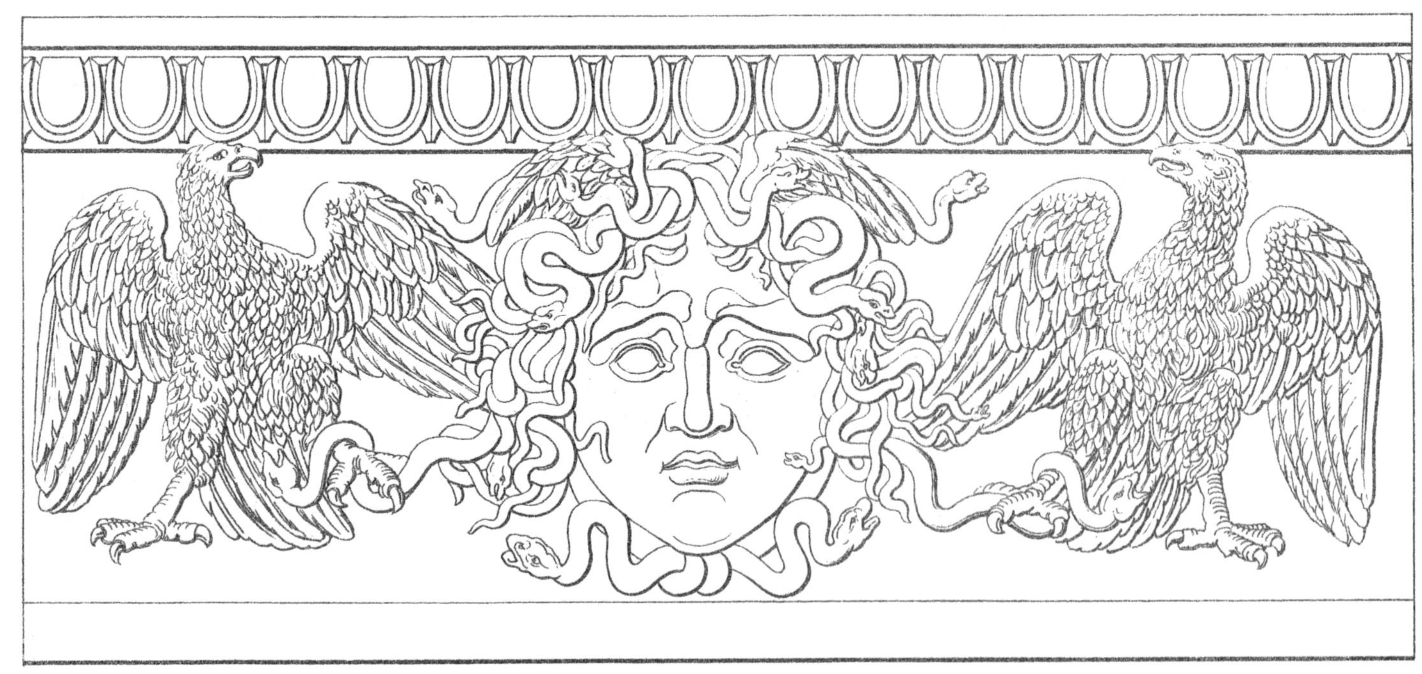

Decorative frieze

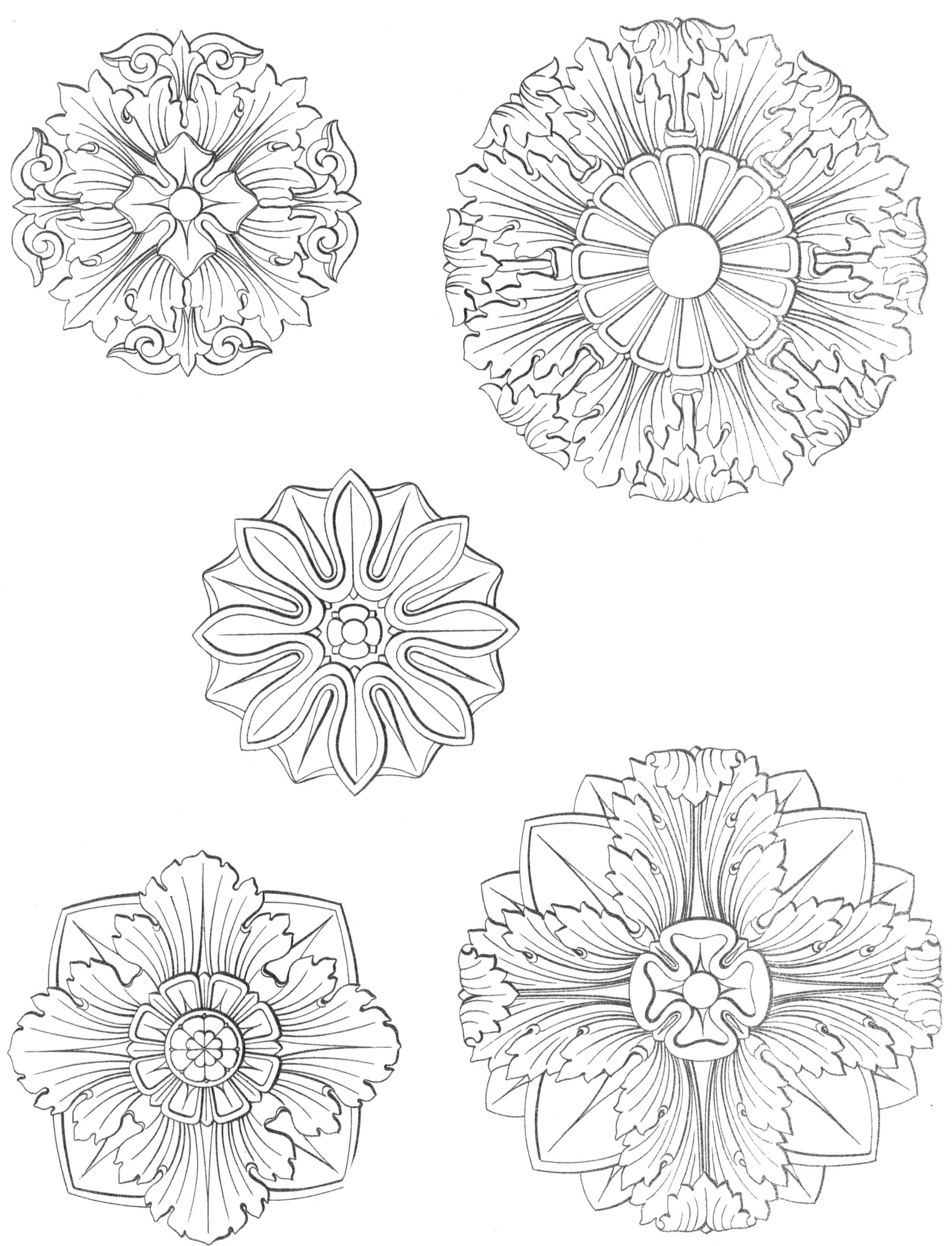

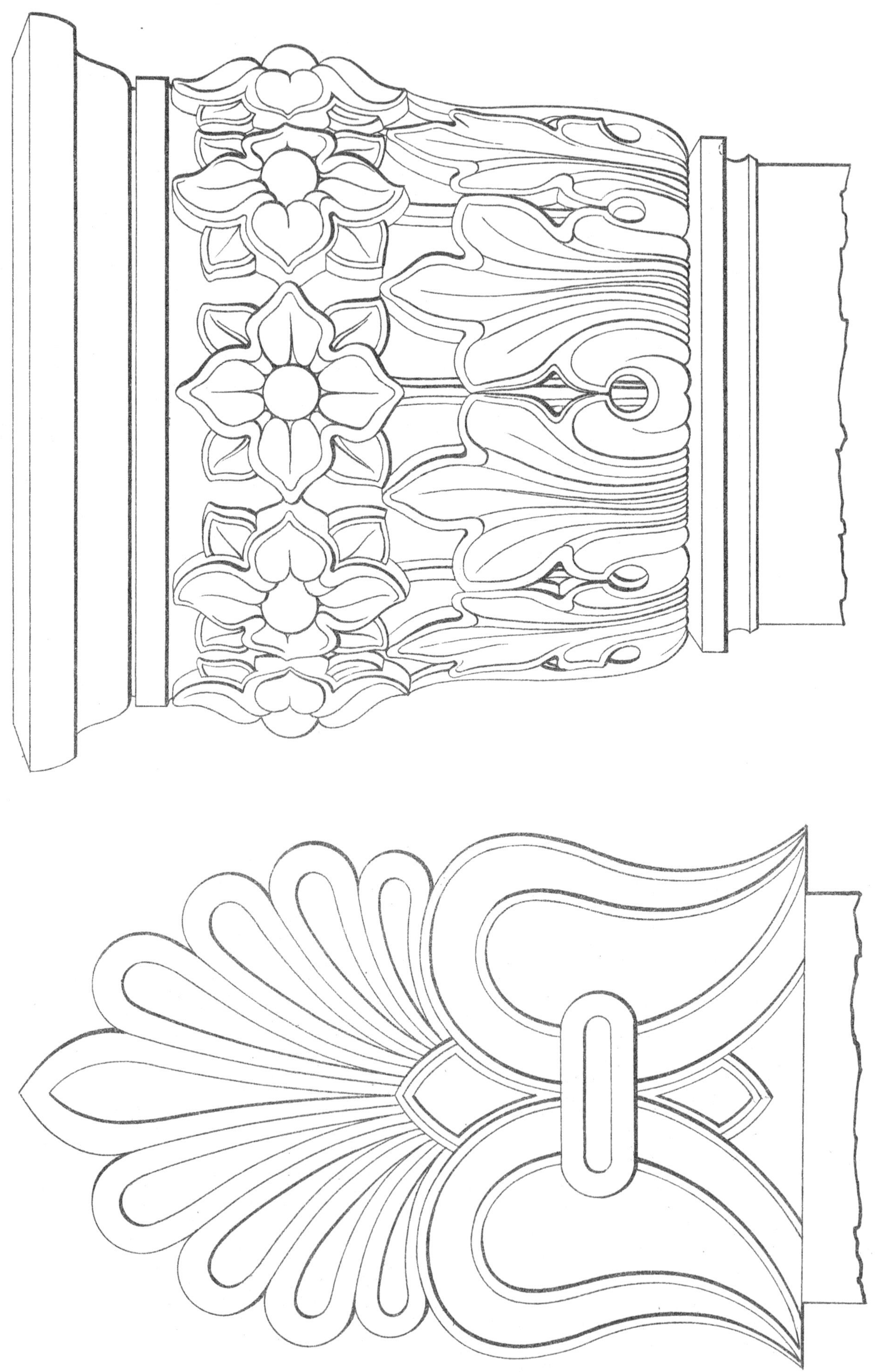

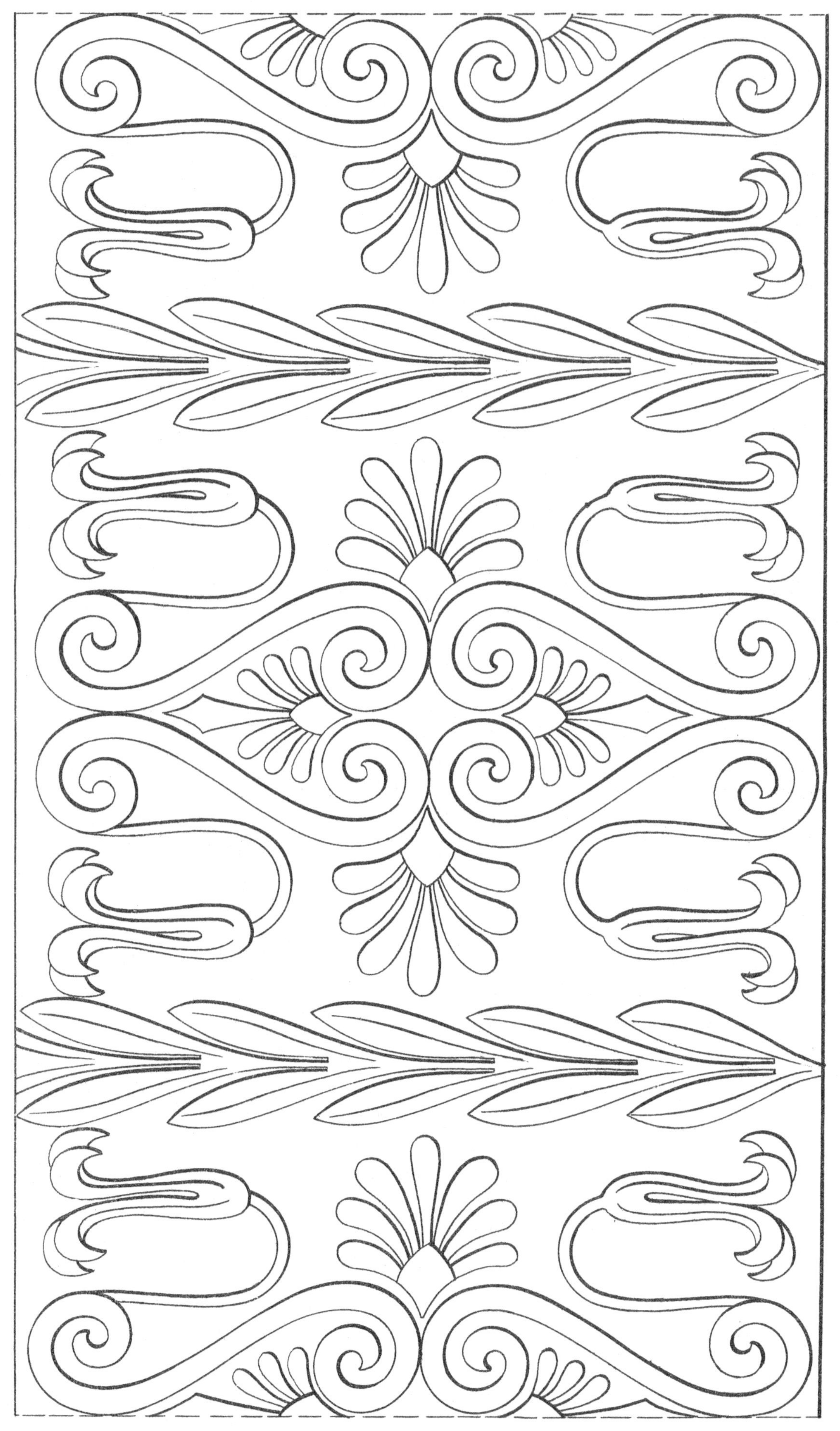

Excavated in Athens in 1838-1839

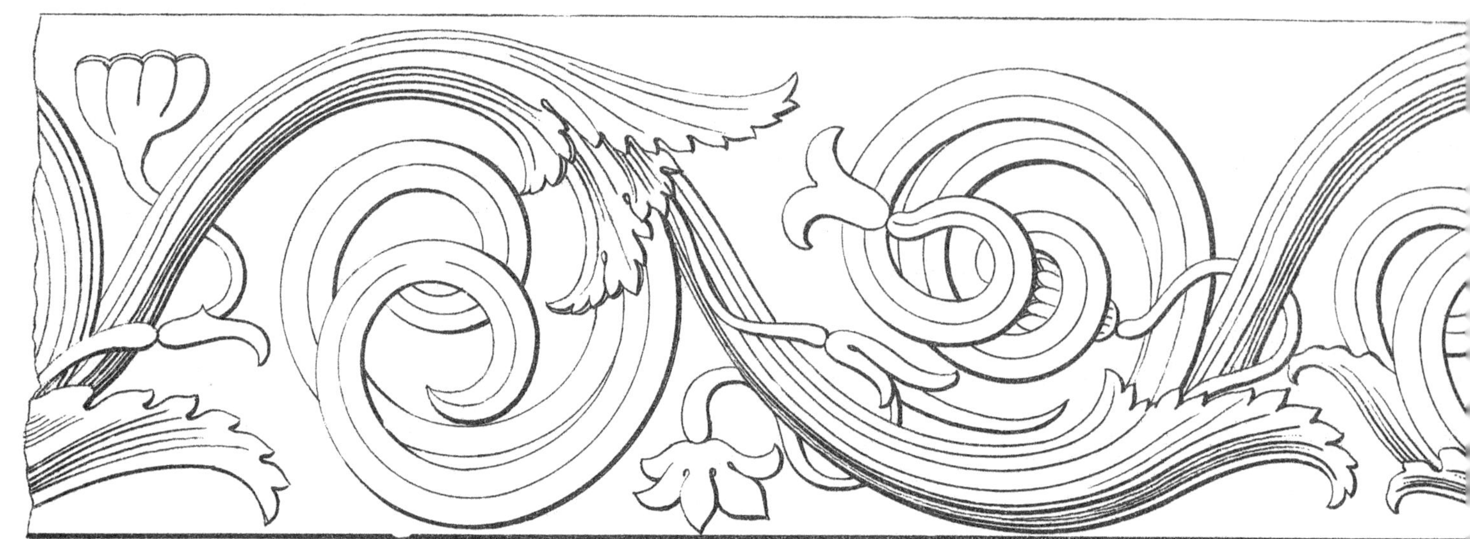

Frieze in the convent of Syriani

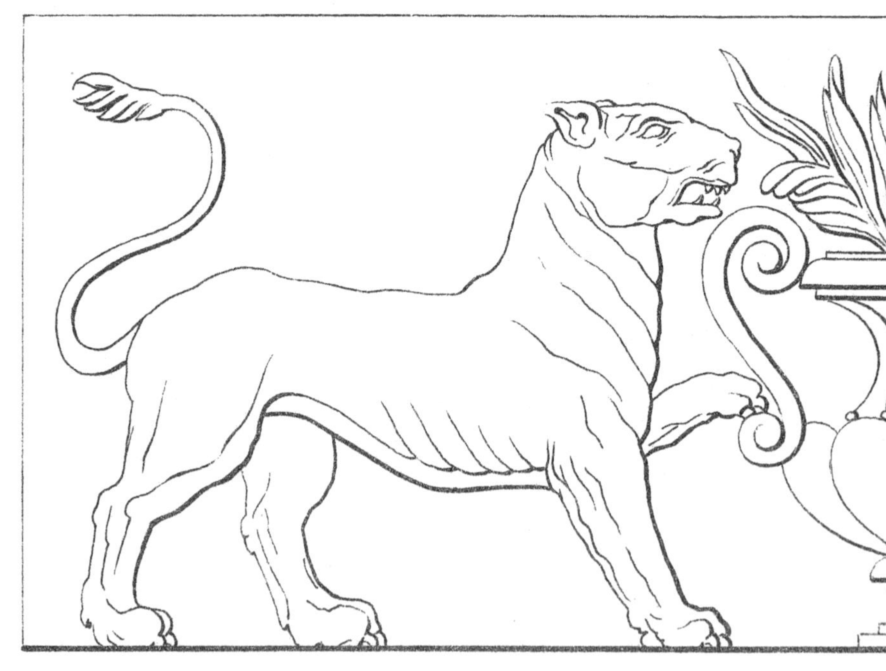

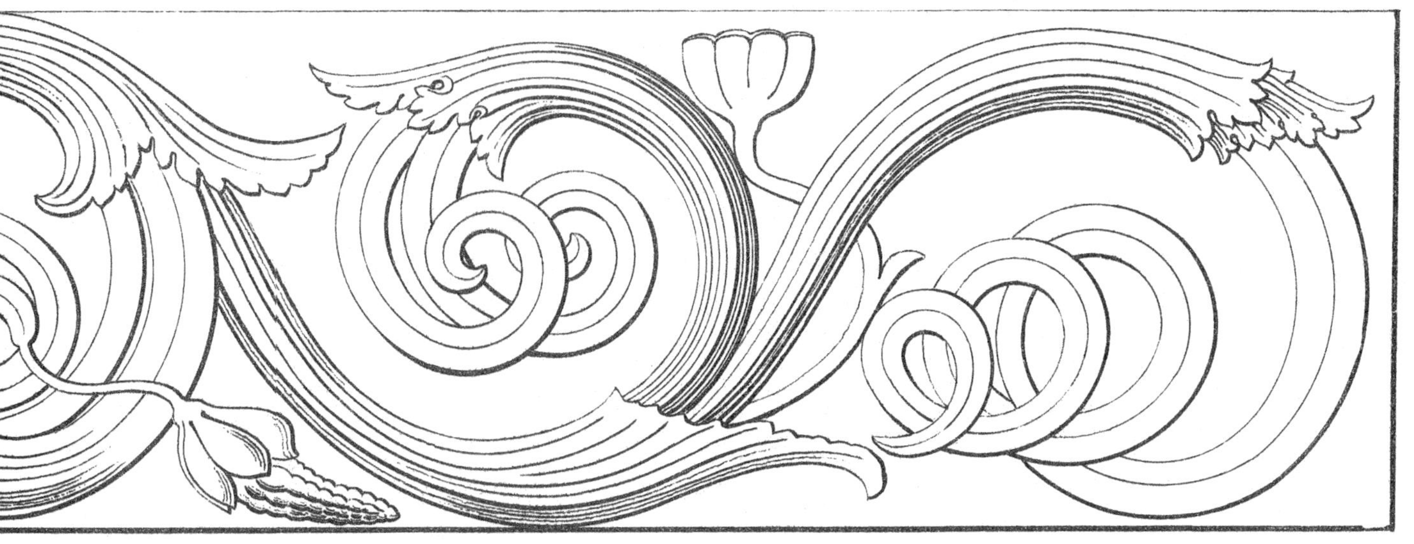

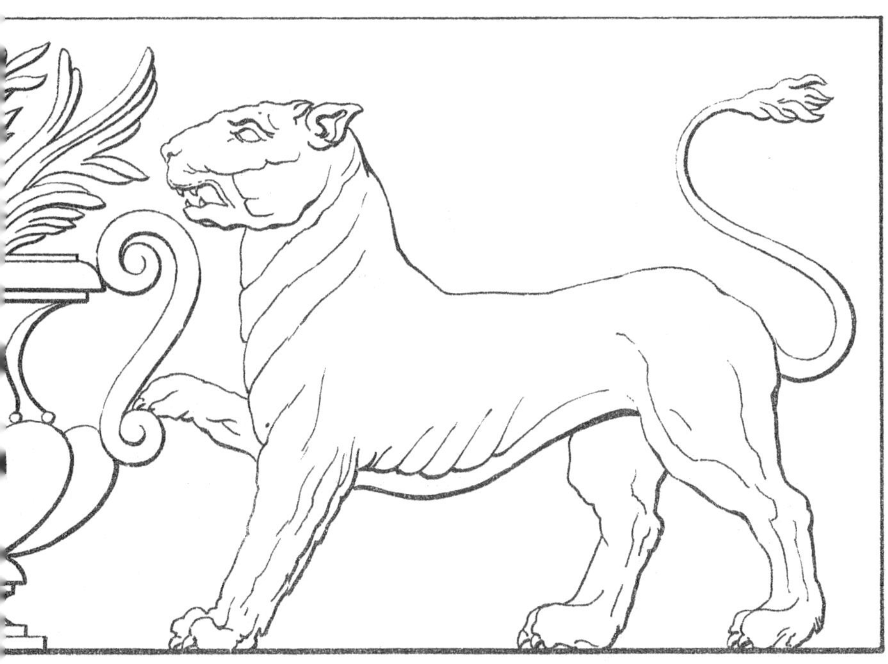

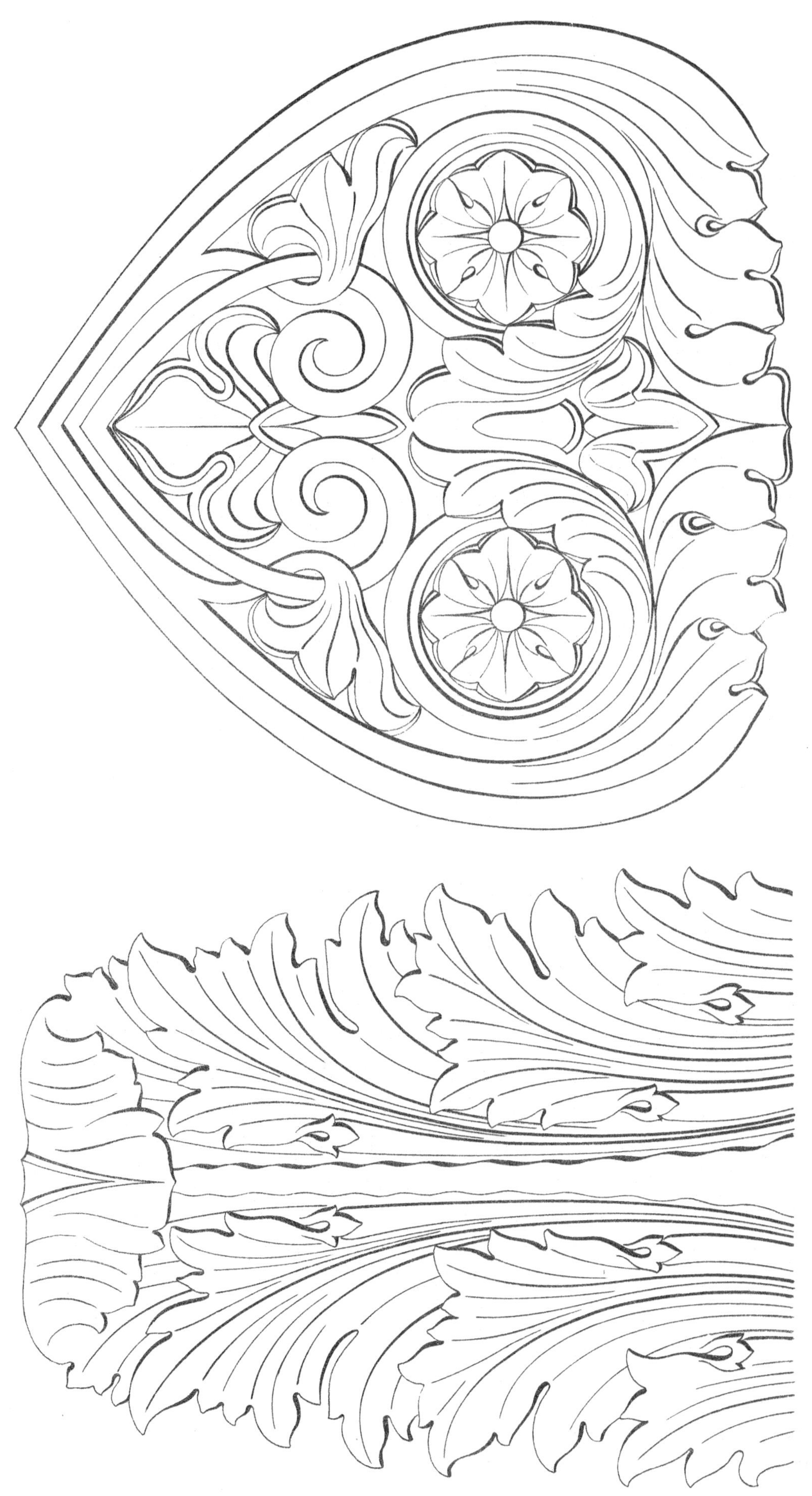

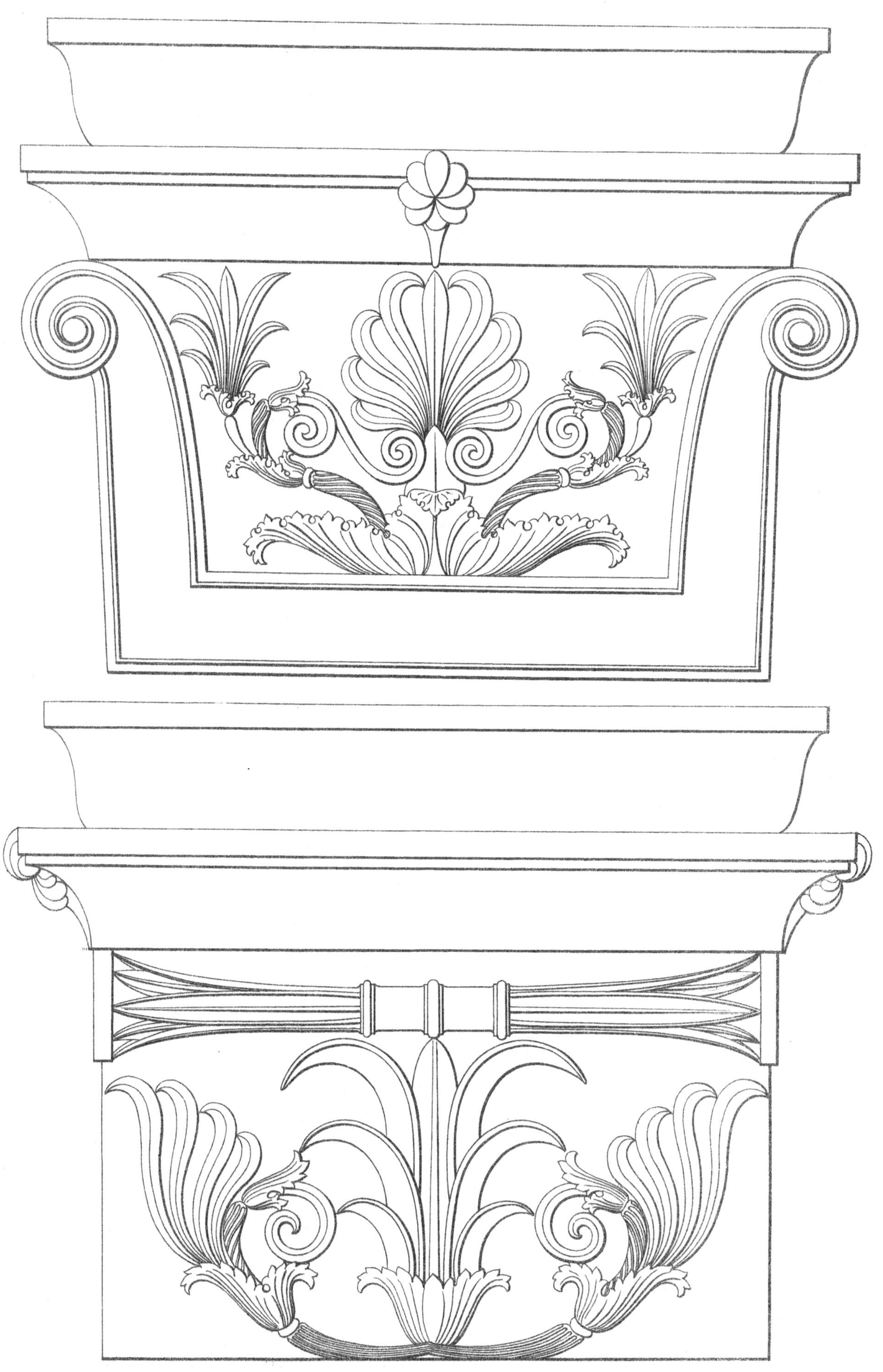

Plate 68

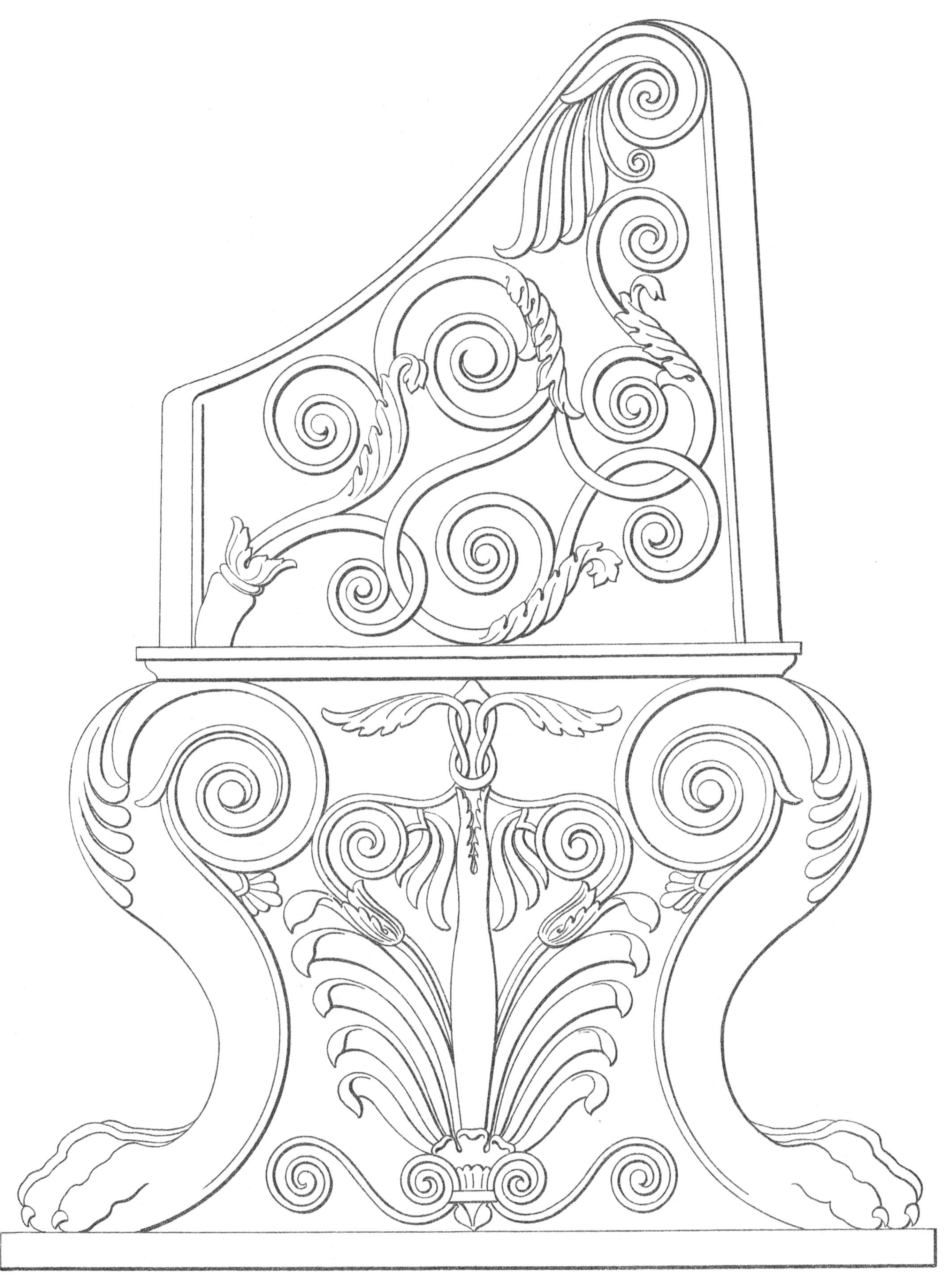

Antique chair

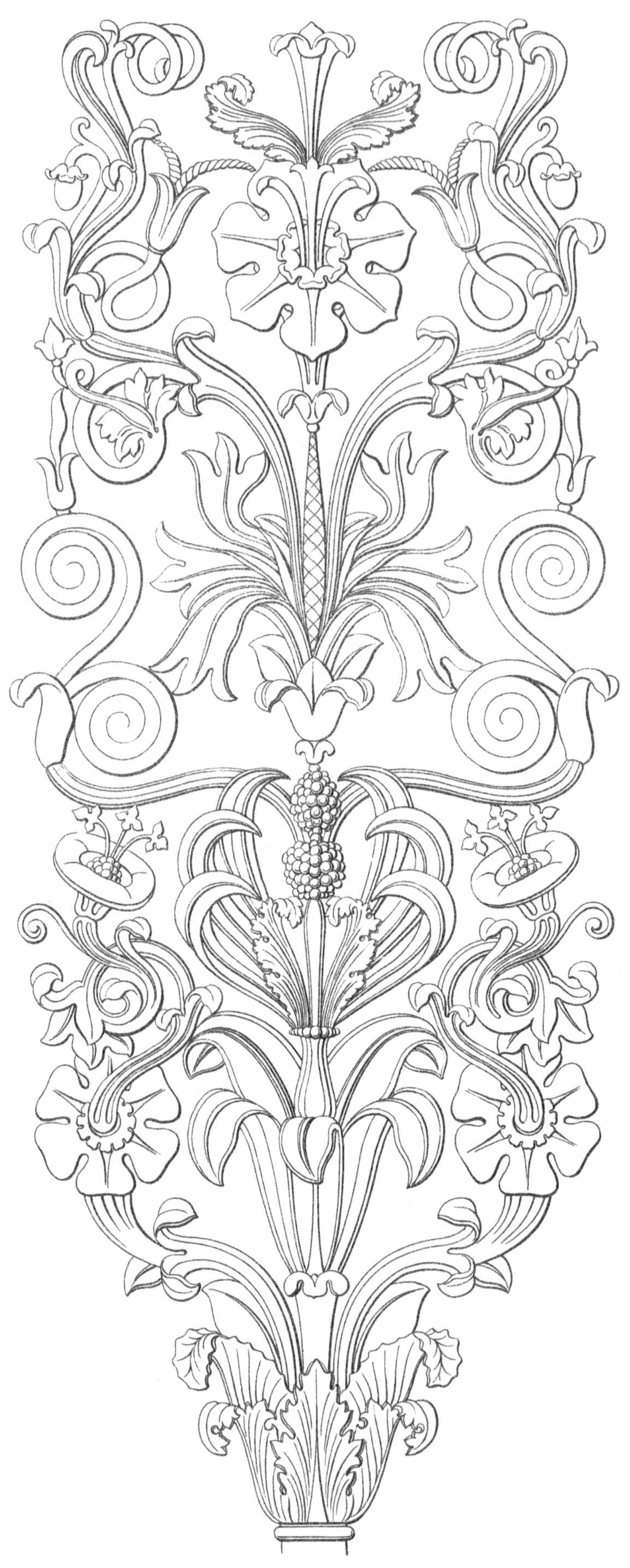

Marble decoration in the Villa Poniatowski in Rome

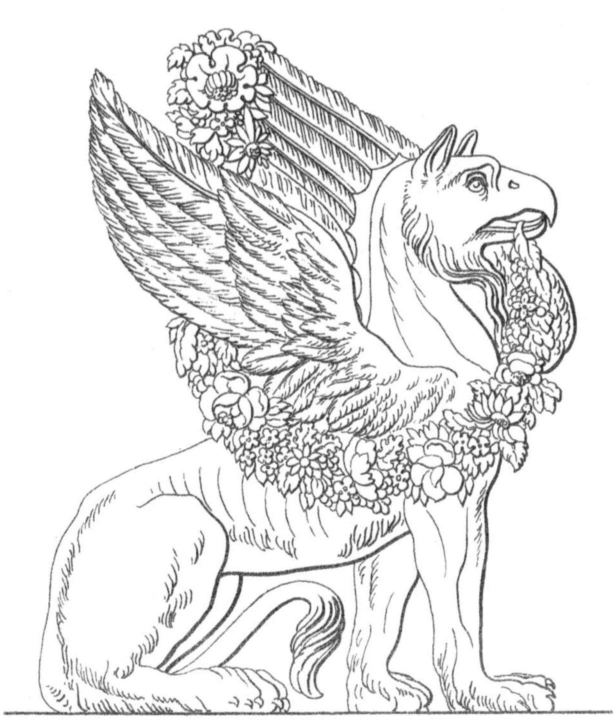

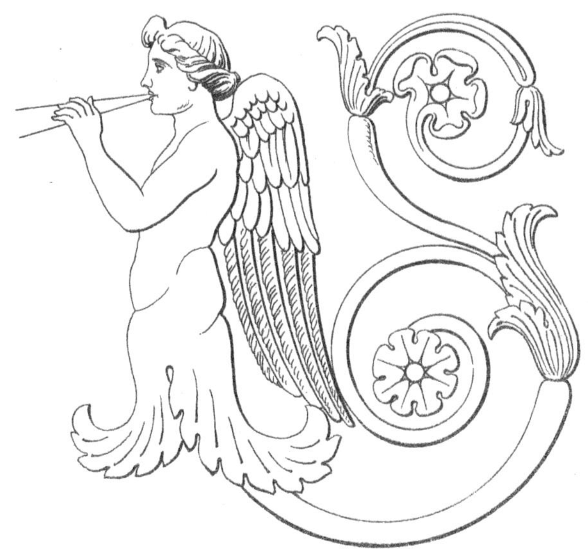

Part of a fragment

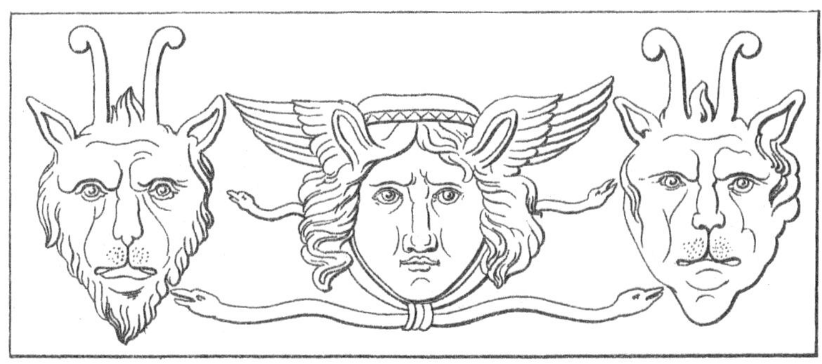

From Herculanum